HOW TO WRITE A PAPER

HOW TO WRITE A PAPER

edited by

GEORGE M HALL

BMJ Publishing Group

First published 1994
Reprinted 1994
Reprinted 1995
Reprinted 1996
Reprinted 1997
by the BMJ Publishing Group
BMA House, Tavistock Square, London WC1H 9JR

British Library Cataloguing in Publication Data
A catalogue record for this book is available from the British Library

ISBN 0–7279–0822–7

Typeset and Printed by Derry and Sons Limited, Nottingham

Contents

Preface

There are many excellent books to help aspiring authors write a scientific paper. Unfortunately they are often written by senior editors or professional medical writers whose links with active research are tenuous, so that they fail to recognise the problems facing beginners. The idea for this book arose from a series of writing workshops for young research workers conducted by the editorial board of the *British Journal of Anaesthesia* in the United Kingdom and abroad. There was a demand for a short book to guide authors, particularly if English was not their first language. The aim of this book is to give simple, didactic advice on how to write a clinical paper. The contributors are drawn from a wide variety of journals and backgrounds, but all are active participants in research or publishing. I am most grateful for the enthusiasm which all authors have brought to this venture.

G M HALL

1 Structure of a scientific paper

GEORGE M HALL

The research you have conducted is obviously of vital importance and must be read by the widest possible audience. It is probably safer to insult a colleague's spouse, family, and driving rather than the quality of his or her research. Fortunately there are now so many medical journals that your chances of not having the work published somewhere are small. Nevertheless the paper must be constructed in the approved manner and presented to the highest possible standards. There is no doubt that editors and assessors look adversely on scruffy manuscripts, regardless of the quality of the science. All manuscripts are constructed in a similar manner, although there are some notable exceptions such as the format used by *Nature*. These exceptions are unlikely to trouble you in the early stages of your research career.

The object of publishing a scientific paper is that you provide a document which contains sufficient information to enable readers to:

- assess the observations you made
- repeat the experiment if they wish
- determine whether the conclusions drawn are justified by the data.

The basic structure of a paper is summarised by the acronym IMRAD, which stands for

Introduction	(What question was asked?)
Methods	(How was it studied?)
Results	(What was found?)
And	
Discussion	(What do the findings mean?)

The following four chapters deal with a specific section of a paper so sections will be described only in outline in this chapter.

Introduction

The introduction should be brief and must state clearly the question that you tried to answer in the study. To lead the reader to this point it is necessary to review briefly the relevant literature.

Many junior authors have difficulties in writing the introduction. The most common problem is the inability to state clearly what question was asked. This should not occur if the study was planned correctly. It is too late to rectify basic errors when attempting to write the paper. Nevertheless, some studies seem to develop a life of their own and the original objectives can easily be forgotten. I find it useful to ask collaborators from time to time what question we hope to answer. If I do not receive a short clear sentence as an answer, then alarm bells ring.

A review of the literature must not appear in the introduction. Only cite those references that are essential to justify your proposed study. Three citations from different groups are usually sufficient to convince most assessors that some fact is "well known" or "well recognised," particularly if the studies are from different countries.

Many research groups write the introduction to a paper before the work is started, but you must never ignore pertinent literature published during the conduct of the study. For example:

It is well known that middle-aged male runners have diffuse brain damage [1,2,3], but whether this was present before running, or arises as a result of repeated cerebral contusions during exercise, has not been established. In the present study we examined cerebral function in a group of sedentary middle-aged men before and after a 6 month exercise programme. Cerebral function was assessed by . . . .

Methods

This important part of the manuscript has become increasingly neglected and yet the methods section is the most common cause of absolute rejection of a paper. If the methods used to try to answer the question were inappropriate, or flawed, then there is no salvation for the work. Chapter 3 contains useful advice about the design of the study and precision of measurement that should be considered when the work is planned, not after the work has been completed.

The main purposes of the methods section are to describe, and sometimes defend, the experimental design and to provide sufficient detail so that a competent worker can repeat the study. The latter is particularly important when you are deciding how much to include in the text. If standard methods of measurement are used then appropriate references are all that is required. In many instances "modifications" of published methods are used and it is these that cause difficulties for other workers. To ensure reproducible data, authors should:

- give complete details of any new methods used
- give the precision of the measurements undertaken
- use statistical analysis sensibly.

The use of statistics is not dealt with in this book. The help of a statistician should be sought at the planning stage of any study. Statisticians are invariably helpful and have contributed greatly to improving both the design and analysis of clinical investigations. They cannot be expected, however, to resurrect a badly designed study.

Results

The results section of a paper has two key features: there should be an overall description of the major findings of the study; and the data should be presented clearly and concisely.

It is not necessary to present every scrap of data that you have collected. There is a great temptation to give all the results, particularly if they were difficult to obtain, but this section should contain only relevant, representative data. The statistical analysis of the results must be appropriate. The easy availability of statistical software packages has not encouraged young research workers to understand the principles involved. The analysis presented must pass what is called in chapter 4 the "Mark I Eyeball Test," sometimes known as the "BOT" (b . . . obvious test). An assessor is only able to estimate the validity of the statistical tests used, so if your analysis is complicated or unusual expect your paper to undergo appraisal by a statistician.

You must strive for clarity in the results section by avoiding unnecessary repetition of data in the text, figures, and tables. It is worthwhile stating briefly what you did *not* find, as this may save other workers in this area from undertaking unnecessary studies.

Discussion

The initial draft of the discussion is almost invariably too long. It is difficult not to write a long, detailed analysis of the literature that you know so well. However, a rough guide to the length of this section is that it should not be more than one third of the total length of the manuscript (Introduction+Methods+Results+ Discussion). Ample scope often remains for further pruning.

Many beginners find this section of the paper difficult. It is possible to compose an adequate discussion around the points in the box.

Writing the discussion
- Summarise the major findings
- Discuss possible problems with the methods used
- Compare your results with previous work
- Discuss the clinical and scientific (if any) implications of your findings
- Suggest further work
- Produce a succinct conclusion

Common errors include repetition of data already given in the results section, the belief that your methods were beyond criticism, and the preferential citing of previous work to suit your conclusions. Good assessors will seize upon such mistakes, so do not even contemplate trying to deceive them.

Although IMRAD describes the basic structure of a paper, there are other important parts of a manuscript. The title, summary (or abstract), and list of authors are described in chapter 6. It is salutary to remember that many people will read the title of the paper, and some will read the summary, but very few will read the complete text. The title and summary of the paper are of great importance for indexing and abstracting purposes, as well as enticements to persuade the reader to peruse the complete text. The use of appropriate references for a paper is described in chapter 7; this is an area commonly full of mistakes. A golden rule is to list only relevant, published references and present them in a manner that is appropriate for the particular journal. The citation of large numbers of references is an indicator of insecurity, not of scholarship. An authoritative author knows the important references that are appropriate to the study.

Before you start the first draft of the manuscript, read carefully the "Instructions to authors" which every journal publishes, and prepare the paper accordingly. Some journals give detailed instructions, often annually, and these can be a valuable way of learning some of the basic rules. It is a grave mistake to submit a paper in the style of another journal; this suggests that it has been rejected recently. At all stages of preparation of the paper, go back and check with the instructions to authors and make sure that your manuscript conforms. It seems very obvious, but if you wish to publish in the *European Annals of Andrology* do not write your paper to conform with the *Swedish Journal of Androgen Research*. Read and re-read the instructions to authors.

Variations on the IMRAD system are sometimes necessary in specialised circumstances, such as a letter to the editor (chapter 8), an abstract for presentation at a scientific meeting (chapter 9), or a case report (chapter 10). Nevertheless, it is a fundamental system that is the basis of all scientific papers.

2 Introductions

RICHARD SMITH

Introductions should be short and arresting and tell the reader why you have undertaken the study. This first sentence tells you almost everything I have to say, and you could stop here. If you were reading a newspaper, you probably would—and that is why journalists writing a news story will try to give the essence of their story in the first line. An alternative technique used by journalists and authors is to begin with a sentence so arresting that the reader will be hooked and likely to stay for the whole piece.

I may mislead by beginning with these journalistic devices, but I want to return to them: scientific writing can usefully borrow from journalism. But let me begin with writing introductions for scientific papers.

Before beginning, answer the basic questions

Before sitting down to write an introduction you must have answered the basic questions that apply to any piece of writing:

- What do I have to say?
- Is it worth saying?
- What is the right format for the message?
- What is the audience for the message?
- What is the right journal for the message?

If you are unclear about the answers to these questions then your piece of writing—no matter whether it's a news story, a poem, or a scientific paper—is unlikely to succeed. As editor of the *British*

Medical Journal, every day I see papers where authors have not answered these questions. Authors are often not clear about what they want to say. They start with some sort of idea and hope that the reader will have the wit to sort out what's important. The reader will not bother. Authors also regularly choose the wrong format—a scientific paper rather than a descriptive essay, or a long paper rather than a short one. Not being clear about the audience is probably the commonest error, and specialists regularly write for generalists in a way that is entirely inaccessible.

Another basic rule is to read the instructions to authors of the journal you are writing for. Too few authors do this, but there is little point in writing a 400 word introduction when the journal has a limit for the whole article of 600 words.

Tell readers why you have undertaken the study

The main job of the introduction is to tell readers why you have undertaken the study. If you set out to answer a question that really interested you, then you will have little difficulty. But if your main reason for undertaking the study was to have something to add to your curriculum vitae, it will show through.

The best questions may arise directly from clinical practice, and if that is the case the introduction should say so:

> A patient came to be anaesthetised for an operation to repair his hernia and asked whether the fact that he used Ecstasy four nights a week would create difficulties. We were unable to find an answer in published medical reports and so designed a study to answer the question.

Or:

> Because of pressure to reduce night work for junior doctors we wondered if it would be safe to delay operating on patients with appendicitis until the morning after they were admitted.

If your audience is interested in the answer to these questions then they may well be tempted to read the paper; and if you have defined your audience and selected the right journal, they should be interested.

More commonly, you will be building on scientific work already published. It then becomes essential to make clear how your work adds importantly to what has gone before.

Clarify what your work adds

Editors will not want to publish—and readers will not want to read—studies that simply repeat what has been done several times before. Indeed, you should not be undertaking a study or writing a paper unless you are confident that it does add importantly to what has gone before. The introduction should not read:

> Several studies have shown that regular Ecstasy use creates anaesthetic difficulties,[1–7] and several others have shown that it does not.[8–14] We report two further patients, one of whom did experience problems and one of whom did not, and review the literature.

Rather it should read something like:

> Two previous studies have reported that regular Ecstasy use may give rise to respiratory problems during anaesthesia. These studies were small and uncontrolled, used only crude measurements of respiratory function, and did not follow up the patients. We report a larger, controlled study, with detailed measurements of respiratory function and two year follow up.

Usually, it is not so easy to make clear how your study is better than what has gone before, and this is where the temptation arises to give a detailed critique of everything that has ever gone before. You will be particularly tempted to do this because if you are serious about your study you will have spent hours in the library detecting and reading every study that has gone before.

The very best introductions will include a systematic review of all the work that has gone before and a demonstration that new work is needed.

The move towards systematic reviews is one of the most important developments in science and scientific writing in the past 20 years.[1] We now understand that most reviews are highly selective in the evidence they adduce and often wrong in the conclusions they reach.[2] When undertaking a systematic review an author poses a clear question, gathers all relevant information (published in whatever language, or unpublished), discards the scientifically weak material, synthesises the remaining information, and then draws a conclusion.

To undertake such a review is clearly a major task, but this ideally is what you should do before you begin a new study. You should then undertake the study only if the question cannot be answered and if your study will contribute importantly to producing an answer. You should include a brief account of the review in the introduction. Readers will then fully understand how your study fits with what has gone before and why it is important.

In 1994 you should not worry that you cannot reach this high standard because the number of medical papers that have ever done so could probably be numbered on the fingers of one hand. But by the end of the millennium brief accounts of such reviews will, I hope, be routine in introductions.

Keep it short

You must resist the temptation to impress readers by summarising everything that has gone before. They will be bored, not impressed, and will probably never make it through your study. Your introduction should not read:

> Archaeologists have hypothesised that a primitive version of Ecstasy may have been widely used in ancient Egypt. Canisters found in tombs of the pharaohs . . . Sociological evidence shows that Ecstasy is most commonly used by males age 15 to 25 at parties held in aircraft hangars . . . The respiratory problems associated with Ecstasy may arise at the alveolar-capillary interface. Aardvark hypothesised in 1926 that problems might arise at this interface because of . . .

Nor should you write:

> Many studies have addressed the problem of Ecstasy and anaesthesia.[1-92]

With such a sentence you say almost nothing useful, and you've promptly filled a whole page with references. You should choose references that are apposite, not simply to demonstrate that you've done a lot of reading.

It may often be difficult to make clear in a few words why your study is superior to what has gone before, but you must convince editors and readers that it is better. Your introduction might read something like:

> Anaesthetists cannot be sure whether important complications may arise in patients who regularly use Ecstasy. Several case studies have described such problems.[1-4] Three cohort studies have been published, two of which found a high incidence of respiratory problems in regular Ecstasy users.

One of these studies was uncontrolled,[5] and in the other the patients were poorly matched for age and smoking.[6] The study that did not find any problems included only six regular Ecstasy users, and the chance of an important effect being missed (a type II error) was high.[7] We have undertaken a study of 50 regular Ecstasy users with controls matched for age, smoking status, and alcohol consumption.

A more detailed critique of the other studies can be left for the discussion. Even then, you should not give an exhaustive account of what has gone before but should concentrate on the best studies that are closest to yours. You will also then be able to compare the strengths and weaknesses of your study with the other studies, something that would be wholly out of place in the introduction.

Make sure that you know what studies have gone before

Editors know that it is easy to miss important earlier studies. Journals may publish studies in which authors proudly give the results of the first study on a problem, only for people to write in saying that they did an identical study 10 years ago. We have certainly had this experience several times at the *British Medical Journal,* and we are always keen to see evidence that authors have made a determined attempt to locate previous studies.

This search should obviously be undertaken before the study is begun, not when it is being written up. It is in nobody's interest to expend time and money answering a question that has already been well answered. Before beginning a study, authors should seek the help of librarians in finding any earlier studies. As well as doing this, authors should also make personal contact with people who are experts in the subject and who may know of published studies that library searches do not find, unpublished studies, or studies currently under way. It's also a good idea to find the latest possible review on the subject and search the references and to look at the abstracts of meetings on the subject. We know that library searches often do not find relevant papers that have already been published, that many good studies remain unpublished (perhaps because they reach negative conclusions), and that studies take years to conduct and sometimes years to get into published reports.

Editors increasingly want to see evidence that authors have worked hard to make sure that they know of studies directly related to theirs. This is particularly important when editors' first reaction to a paper is

"Surely we know this already." We regularly have this experience at the *British Medical Journal*, and we then look especially hard to make sure that authors have put effort into finding what has gone before.

In a systematic review (or meta-analysis) the search strategy clearly belongs in the methods section, but in an ordinary paper it belongs in the introduction—in as short a form as possible. Thus it might read:

> A Medline search using 15 different key phrases, personal contact with five experts in the subject, and a personal search of five recent conferences on closely related subjects produced no previous studies of whether grandmothers suck eggs.

Be sure your readers are convinced of the importance of your question, but don't overdo it

If you have selected the right audience and a good study then you should not have to work hard to convince your readers of the importance of the question you are answering. One common mistake is to start repeating material that is in all the textbooks and that your readers will know. Thus, in a paper on whether vitamin D will prevent osteoporosis you do not need to tell your readers what osteoporosis and vitamin D are. You might, however, want to give them a sense of the scale of the problem by giving prevalence figures for osteoporosis, data on hospital admissions related to osteoporosis, and figures on the costs to the nation of the problem.

Don't baffle your readers

Although you don't want to patronise and bore your readers by telling them things that they already know, you certainly don't want to baffle them by introducing, without explanation, material that is wholly unfamiliar. Nothing turns readers off faster than abbreviations that mean nothing or references to diseases, drugs, reports, places, or whatever, that they do not know. This point simply emphasises the importance of knowing your audience.

Give the study's design but not the conclusion

This is a matter of choice, but I ask authors to give a one sentence description of their study at the end of their introduction. The last line might read:

We therefore conducted a double blind randomised study with 10 year follow up to determine whether teetotallers drinking three glasses of whisky a week can reduce their chances of dying of coronary artery disease.

I don't like it, however, when the introduction also gives the final conclusion:

Drinking three glasses of whisky a week does not reduce teetotallers' chances of dying of coronary artery disease.

Other editors may think differently.

Think about using journalistic tricks sparingly

The difficult part of writing is to get the structure right. Spinning sentences is much easier, and editors can much more easily change sentences than structure. Most pieces of writing that fail do so because the structure is poor, and that is why writing scientific articles is comparatively easy—the structure is given to you.

I have assumed in this chapter that you are writing a scientific paper. If you are writing something else you will have to think much harder about the introduction and about the structure of the whole piece. But even if you are writing a scientific paper you might make use of the devices that journalists use to hook their readers.

Tim Albert, a medical journalist, gives five possible openings in his excellent book on medical journalism[3]: telling an arresting story; describing a scene vividly; using a strong quotation; giving some intriguing facts; or making an opinionated and controversial pronouncement. He gives two examples from the health page of the *Independent*. Mike Handscomb wrote:

In many respects it is easier and less uncomfortable to have leukaemia than eczema . . .

This is an intriguing statement, and readers will be interested to read on to see if the author can convince them that his statement contains some truth. Or Jeremy Laurance began a piece:

This is a story of sex, fear, and money. It is about a new treatment for an embarrassing problem which could prove a money spinner in the new commercial National Health Service . . .

Sex, fear, and money are emotive to all of us and we may well want to know how a new treatment could make money for the health service rather than cost it money.

My favourite beginning occurs in Anthony Burgess's novel *Earthly Powers*. The first sentence reads:

> It was the afternoon of my eighty-first birthday, and I was in bed with my catamite when Ali announced that the archbishop had come to see me.

This starts the book so powerfully that it might well carry us right through the next 400 or so pages.

To begin a paper in the *British Journal of Anaesthesia* with such a sentence would be to court rejection, ridicule, and disaster, but some of the techniques advocated by Tim Albert could be used. I suggest, however, staying away from opinionated statements and quotations in scientific papers—particularly if they come from Shakespeare, the Bible, or *Alice in Wonderland*.

Conclusion

To write an effective introduction you must know your audience, keep it short, tell readers why you have done the study and explain why it's important, convince them that it is better than what has gone before, and try as hard as you can to hook them in the first line.

[1] Chalmers I. Improving the quality and dissemination of reviews of clinical research. In: Lock S, ed. *The future of medical journals*. London: BMJ, 1991: 127–48.

[2] Mulrow CD. The medical review article: state of the science. *Ann Intern Med* 1987; **104**: 485–8.

[3] Albert T. *Medical journalism: the writer's guide*. Oxford: Radcliffe, 1992.

3 Methods

G B DRUMMOND

The methods section should describe, in logical sequence, how the study was designed and carried out, and how the data were analysed. After the study has been done, this is often a relatively simple task. Sadly, at this stage you may recognise unfortunate weaknesses in your study, particularly in the design. Consequently, although it may be difficult, you would do better to write this part of the paper in as much detail as possible *before* the study has started. An experienced colleague can then look through this description so that weaknesses may be detected. The intellectual challenge of setting down what is to be done is also a very useful practical exercise; much better than finding out after months of hard work that "you should have started out from somewhere else," or measured an extra variable, or finding that a predictable need had not been anticipated and catered for in advance.

Testing hypotheses

When readers turn to the methods section, they often wish to find out much more than merely which apparatus was used. They want to know exactly what hypothesis was tested. A simple hypothesis might be that an intervention should result in a particular effect, such as an increase in survival or improvement in outcome. This is tested by assuming a null hypothesis, that the intervention is ineffective, and then assessing how possible it would be for the observed results to occur if this null hypothesis were indeed correct. The expression of how small the possibility (p value) has to be to disprove the null hypothesis should be stated clearly as the "mission statement" of the study. Thus, a study of two antibiotics might compare cure rate: the reader would infer that the null hypothesis was that there was no difference with regard to cure. A p value of less than 0·05 (out of a total probability of 1) implies that a value less than this will disprove the null hypothesis. Many papers merely say, adequately, "$p<0·05$ was considered significant".

The other side of the coin of probability, often neglected, is the *power* of the study. Readers should not be encouraged to believe that if the null hypothesis survives, there is no significant difference between the groups. It is not necessarily so: the study has merely failed to destroy the null hypothesis. The negative outcome may be true, but it could be false. For example, a true difference could exist, but it might only be small. The variability of the measurements could be large, so that although a large difference is present it fails to be significant. The reader can assess this possibility if you give an estimate of the power of the study, as designed and executed, in your description of the methods. This is expressed as the β error. β is the possibility of a false negative conclusion. The appropriate value of β that you may choose will vary according to the precision of the answer needed and the practical consequences of an incorrect conclusion. Commonly it is taken to be 0·2. The actual value of β varies with the size of the difference considered important, the variability of the data, and the size of the study.

Always try to state clearly the a priori hypotheses, if only to ensure that you collect appropriate and relevant data, and that you do the correct statistical tests.

Statistics

Give the exact tests used to analyse the data statistically, with an appropriate reference if the test is not well known. If a computer was used, then give the type of computer, the software, and the software version. The choice of statistical test depends on the type of data. It may not be clear before the data are collected if parametric tests can be used, in which case the a priori tests should be non-parametric.

Design

The study design can often be described in a few well chosen words, particularly if it is a description of a layout of the groups or events. The groups may be *independent*, allocated to different

15

treatments, and the design is often *parallel*, each group receiving a different treatment, with both groups being entered at the same time. In this case comparisons will be between groups. Subjects receiving different treatments may be *paired*, to reduce the effects of confounding variables such as weight or sex. The effects of a treatment on each subject may be assessed before and after; such comparisons are *within subject*. The simplest study design is a *randomised parallel design* with a comparison of outcome between groups.

What to include in the methods section

How the study was designed:
- Keep the description brief
- Say how randomisation was done
- Use names to identify parts of a study sequence

How the study was carried out:
- Describe how the subjects were recruited and chosen
- Give reasons for excluding subjects
- Consider mentioning ethical features
- Give accurate details of materials used
- Give exact drug dosages
- Give the exact form of treatment and accessible details of unusual apparatus

How the data were analysed:
- Use a p value to disprove the null hypothesis
- Give an estimate of the power of the study (the likelihood of a false negative—the β error)
- Give the exact tests used for statistical analysis (chosen a priori)

Always state clearly how randomisation was done, since this is a crucial part of many clinical trials. The method used should be stated explicitly in this section. Specific aspects such as blocked randomisation (to obtain roughly similar group sizes) and stratification (to obtain a balance of confounding variables such as age or sex in each group) must be described. Authors often choose wrong forms of randomisation such as alternate cases, the unit number, date of birth, and so on. Correct methods involve the use of random number tables or closed envelope methods. In a study that involves blind assessment you may need to describe how the assessor was kept unaware of the treatment allocation.

A diagram may be helpful if the design of the study is complex, or a complicated sequence of interventions is carried out. You can help

16

readers by using explicit names for the separate parts of a study sequence so that they can follow the results; names or even initials are preferable to indicate groups or events rather than calling these events 3, 4, 5, and so on.

Subjects and materials

Readers want to know how the subjects were recruited and chosen. Healthy, non-pregnant (probably male) volunteers may not reflect the clinical circumstances of many occasions when a drug is used. Try to give an indication of what disease states have been excluded, and how these diseases were defined and diagnosed. What medication leads to exclusion from the study? Alcohol and tobacco use can alter drug responses, and it is tempting to exclude subjects who drink and smoke, but the results are less applicable to clinical practice. A list of the inclusion and exclusion criteria set out in the ethics application form may be helpful.

Although most journals indicate that ethical approval is a prerequisite for acceptance, some ethical features of study design may need to be mentioned. For example, you may need to describe some of the practical problems of obtaining informed consent, or of obtaining a satisfactory comparative treatment.

In a laboratory study, details such as the source and strain of animals, bacteria, or other biological material, or the raw materials used, are necessary to allow comparisons to be made with other studies and so that others could repeat the study you have described. Give exact drug dosages (generic name, chemical formula if not well known, and proprietary preparation used if relevant) and how you prepared solutions, with their precise concentrations.

The exact form of treatment used has to be described in a way to allow replication. If the methods, devices, or techniques are widely known, or can be looked up in a standard text—the random zero sphygmomanometer, or a Vitalograph spirometer, for example—then further information is unnecessary. Similarly, widely used apparatus such as the Fleisch pneumotachograph does not require further description, but less well known apparatus should be described by giving the name, type, and manufacturer.

Methods that are likely to be uncommon or unique should be described fully or an adequate reference to the method should be provided. Readers object if a reference of this sort is only to an abstract or a limited description in a previous paper. If in doubt, provide details and indicate how the methods were validated.

The apparatus used must be described in sufficient detail to allow the reader to be confident of the results reported. Is the apparatus appropriate, sensitive enough, specific in its measurement, reproducible, and accurate? Each aspect may need to be considered separately. For example, bathroom scales may fulfil all these criteria when used to estimate human body weight, as long as they have been checked and calibrated recently. On the other hand an inadequate chemical assay may be non-specific because it responds to other substances, gives different results when the same sample is tested twice (poor reproducibility), and gives results that are consistently different from the value expected when tested against a standard substance (poor accuracy). The method may not detect low concentrations (insufficient sensitivity).

The methods used to standardise, calibrate, and assess the linearity and frequency response of the measuring devices used may need to be described. Such characteristics should be given when high fidelity measurements are reported. Do not merely repeat the manufacturer's data for accuracy of a piece of apparatus, particularly if it is crucial to the study: the standard used for a calibration must be stated and the results of the calibration quoted. If analogue to digital conversion is done in computerised analysis, an indication of the sampling rate and accuracy of sampling procedure is necessary. Similar considerations of adequate description apply to other methods of assessment and follow up, such as questionnaires, which should be validated.

A good methods section can answer these questions

- Does the text describe what question was being asked, what was being tested, and how trustworthy the measurements of the variable under consideration would be?
- Were these trustworthy measurements recorded, analysed, and interpreted correctly?
- Would a suitably qualified reader be able to repeat the experiment in the same way?

4 The results

JOHN NORMAN

The results section is where you provide the answers to the questions you posed in the introduction. These answers will most likely be the ones you were expecting. Occasionally they won't be and you will refute your original ideas. A further set of answers may occur to questions you were not expecting to answer. Serendipity has a part to play.

What you will have to avoid is what any editor or assessor dreads to see: "The results are presented in tables I to V and in the figures." Not only does that not guide your readers into discovering what you want them to find, but it actively encourages them to find out what you do not want them to discover. You must lead readers into following your thoughts. You do this by using a mixture of text, tables, and illustrations.

You will need to describe the subjects of your investigation with enough detail for the reader to assess how normal or abnormal they are. You might have given this detail in the methods section, but it is common for the first part of the results section to show the nature and comparability of any groups of subjects you have studied.

The next sections present the answers and again a mixture of text, tables, and illustrations may well be needed. In general, readers will follow the text as though reading a story—they start at the beginning and work in one dimension towards the end. So—tell the story. The tables usually present the meat of the results and will establish the statistical validity of your conclusions. They may be brief or full—it will depend on what you are going to show.

Illustrations fill a number of roles. You may want to show a photograph or a micrograph. Or you may want to use a record from some polygraph to show an example of the results you find. These are helpful especially to those readers who are working in the same field. You might want to construct a figure which illustrates the statistical conclusions—the mind will pick up trends and associations very much more easily with a well constructed figure than it will by reading the text or the tables. But do remember if the actual numbers are not in the text or the tables an awkward assessor will count the number of dots you have plotted on your regression figure or, worse, will measure the size of your standard error bars and then dispute your statistical conclusions. Don't give the assessor that chance. Include all types of presentations if they are needed.

The words

Tell the story of how you arrived at your answers. Establish initially how normal or abnormal your study groups were and how comparable they were. Even if you have randomly allocated your subjects into groups, remember to show the groups are comparable. With two groups there is a 1:20 chance that a random allocation will produce groups that differ significantly (statistically) in some way. Many journals print 20 papers in each issue—yours may be the unlucky one. If it does happen, you will have to comment and state, in the discussion, how that might have affected the significance of the results.

Having established your study baseline you might want to discuss a typical response. Describe the example even if you are also using an illustration. The reader will understand that your typical response is likely to be your most dramatic result. But we are all human! Then summarise in the text the answer to your main question. I hope your results will be in line with your expectations and the evidence will support your hypothesis. Give an indication of the size of any differences you have found in your study groups and the statistical significance of these differences. You will discuss later the differences between statistical and practical significance. If your results do not support your original idea, or even refute it, then you will need to describe the differences and the statistical significance. Remember that Sir Karl Popper is the great advocate of learning by refuting hypotheses. Confirmatory results may support your ideas but results that go against them will make you, and your reader, think again and come up with a better idea or, possibly, a reason why your results did not conform to prediction.

You almost certainly will find some unexpected results in your study. The final part of the results section will introduce these, illustrate them, and give their statistical significance. This area will need development in the discussion to assess what the results mean and what should be done in the future.

The statistics

Many papers suffer because the statistics are presented badly. There are many statistical tests that can be used. You will have planned your study to include the statistical tests you will use. You will not have taken the results to your local statistician to see what can be made of them. Bad planning leads to poor results and a waste of everyone's time. But even with the right tests it is not easy to condense the results into the space available in a paper. Try!

In general do not give results to a greater degree of accuracy than that of the measurement. If you can only measure cardiac output with an accuracy of $\pm$ 10% do not quote values for individual results to three significant figures. The convention for describing means does allow you to use one more significant figure than for your individual results (as you may also for standard deviations and errors). Take care that any statistically significant changes you want to emphasise are greater than your errors of measurement.

If you are looking at proportions of the groups with various attributes, avoid using percentages unless the groups contain more than 100 subjects.

Often in the text and the tables you will be unable to present all your data. You must condense, but not to an extent that the reader (and assessor and editor) cannot follow you. Suppose you have 100 subjects and you have measured some characteristic—perhaps the weight of each patient. Rather than give the full 100 results you must condense. You will need to give the number of subjects studied, the range of results found, some measure of the central tendency, and some measure of the spread. Spread is often measured by the probability of where the mean value lies in the whole population, but you might need to use a measure of spread of the whole population. If the data follow a normal distribution you can use the mean and either the standard error of the mean or the standard deviation. The current popular measure of the spread is the confidence interval for the mean. Choose your set according to the answer you want to give. For a non-normal distribution you might want to use a transformation to make the data fit a normal distribution (logarithms, for example). Alternatively, you can use the median and its confidence interval and the quartiles. Give as much information as you can in as small a space as possible.

Often the results you wish to highlight may be a series of measurements of variables such as arterial pressure or plasma hormone concentrations at various times and you want to show where the significant events occur. Your tables of results may present summaries of these as means and confidence intervals or standard errors. Your statistical analysis may have been an analysis of variance—possibly even a two way analysis. You should present the table for the analysis showing the estimates of variance with their associated degrees of freedom and the F values. If you do not, the assessor will use the much cruder t test to check your conclusions and that may lead to a delay until you sort matters out. With such complex techniques there is a case for including with your paper an extra table of all the results but marked as being for editorial and assessors' use only. They can check your conclusions with their tests. You can offer to let the readers have these data if they write to you. If your statistical analysis is esoteric and not given in full, the assessor will use the "Mark I Eyeball Test" on your results. Be prepared for a discussion that will delay publication.

Guidelines for presenting results

- Use a mixture of text, tables, and figures
- Give the actual numbers of results that are plotted
- Establish how comparable your groups were
- Describe the unexpected results also
- Do not give results to a greater degree of accuracy than that of the measurement
- Avoid using percentages unless the groups have more than 100 subjects
- When condensing results give the number of subjects, the range of results, the central tendency (mean ±SD), and the spread (confidence interval for the mean)
- If you have done an analysis of variance give the estimates with their degrees of freedom and F values
- Tables and illustrations should have an appropriate legend and stand alone
- Prepare tables and figures according to the journal's instructions to authors
- Don't get carried away with computer graphics if they do not add anything

There are similar problems if you are looking at associations between variables. The statistical significance needs to be brought out to emphasise how much of the association can be directly attributed to the dependence of one variable on the other and how much is due to chance. You might need to present measures of the degree of confidence with which you make the associations. Beware of extrapolations. Here you will have discussed these matters with your statistician and made the right choices in the planning stage.

Statistical presentation is always a problem—there is so much information and so little space. But do present enough for the intelligent reader to believe what you are saying.

The tables

You can present a vast amount of detail in the tables which accompany the text. In general do not use the tables you have prepared to accompany your talk on your project—those are designed for rapid assimilation by the audience and will rarely have more than five rows and columns in them. (If they have, you should have been shot down at the talk!)

The key is to make each table deal with a specific problem. The first may well describe the characteristics of your groups. Do not call these "demographics"—according to the *Shorter Oxford Dictionary*, demography is the branch of anthropology studying the statistics of births, deaths, and diseases. The other tables will present your results—those of the actual measurements and those of the calculations from them.

If you have a lot of data then you may need large tables. If you want readers to look at changes in any one characteristic remember that they will usually read from left to right and not from top to bottom. So present the results in columns where the changes run across from one column to the next. Mark those changes where there are statistically significant results. Remember that if there is much information (say a table of 11 columns and 10 rows) there is a strong chance that you will find statistically significant results—especially if you have used a multiple t test. If you want to present results as percentage changes from initial conditions then you ought to present an initial column of what those conditions were. Expressing them as 100% can hide some important differences.

TABLE 1 Summarised results on pretraumatic and trauma related headache

Pretraumatic headache

	n (%)
No	63 (54)
Yes	54 (46)

Type of pretraumatic headache

	n (%)
Migraine	15 (28)
Tension type	19 (35)
Cervicogenic	4 (7)
Non-specified	16 (30)
Total	54 (100)

Frequency of pretraumatic headache

	n (%)
At least once a week	36 (67)
Less than weekly	18 (33)
Total	54 (100)

Trauma-related headache

		Pretraumatic headache		n (%)	
		No	Yes		
		32	18		
T1	No	32	18	50 (43)	Chi-square= 3.55, p=0.059
	Yes	31	36	67 (57)	
T2	No	48	28	76 (65)	Chi-square= 7.94, p=0.004
	Yes	15	26	41 (35)	
T3	No	56	30	86 (73)	Chi-square= 15.67, p<0.0001
	Yes	7	24	31 (27)	

Distribution of trauma-related headache during follow-up

								n
T1	No	Yes	Yes	No	No	No	Yes	Yes	67
T2	No	No	Yes	No	Yes	Yes	No	Yes	41
T3	No	No	No	Yes	No	Yes	Yes	Yes	31
	39 (33)	33 (28)	12 (10)	4 (3)	2 (2)	5 (4)	0 (0)	22 (19)	

Table submitted for publication.

TABLE I Association between pretraumatic headache and trauma related headache in patients with common whiplash injury

Time of assessment	Presence of trauma related headache	Presence of pretraumatic headache		No (%) of patients	χ^2, p Value
		No	Yes		
Baseline	No	32	18	50 (43)	3.55, 0.059
	Yes	31	36	67 (57)	
Three months	No	48	28	76 (65)	7.94, 0.004
	Yes	15	26	41 (35)	
Six months	No	56	30	86 (73)	15.67, <0.0001
	Yes	7	24	31 (27)	

*Percentages refer to whole sample (n=117)

TABLE II Distribution of trauma related headache during follow up in patients with common whiplash injury

Presence of headache at baseline/three months/ six months*	No (%) of patients
No/no/no	39 (33)
Yes/no/no	33 (28)
No/yes/no	2 (2)
Yes/yes/no	12 (10)
No/no/yes	4 (3)
Yes/no/yes	0
No/yes/yes	5 (4)
Yes/yes/yes	22/19

*Number of patients at baseline, three months, and six months were 67, 41, and 31 respectively.

Data in table on p24 presented more clearly in two smaller tables

Make your presentation in the tables match your statistical evaluation. Do not present means and standard errors if you have used a statistical test based on non-parametric methods. This only annoys. Ensure you are using the minimum number of significant figures. This is vital if your number (such as systemic vascular resistance) is calculated from a number of other measurements (mean arterial pressure, venous pressure, and cardiac output) and may have errors which sum those of the individual measurements. This applies especially when the computer has been used for the results. Computers necessarily work with a large number of significant digits if errors are not to occur: the problem is that the output can greatly exceed the value of the input.

One final point. Use the instruction to authors to ensure that the style of the table you make is the same as that of the journal. Use horizontal lines to separate title material and the various sections. Few journals use vertical lines, so although your word processing pack may produce tables with boxes (combinations of horizontal and vertical lines) do not use this form. Always check your final draft with a recent copy of the journal to ensure you are using the right style. The possibility of saving editorial time might just influence the editor in favour.

The illustrations

A picture is worth a thousand words—if it is a good one. The mind takes in visual presentations remarkably well where it will find difficulties with words. Good illustrations will display the data and lead the reader to think about the substance of the answers you have found, and they can reveal the data at several levels. Tufte's book *(The Visual Display of Quantitative Information)* is a marvellous guide to what should be done with the illustrations. Only some key points can be given here. One of the most important is to remember that your illustrations will almost certainly have been through one photographic process to go to the editor. An editor will have them processed again before producing the film for reproduction in the journal. Although film carries a vast amount of detail, each stage of reproduction introduces some loss of quality. Make your originals of as high a quality as possible.

The excellent pictures you made for your talk to the learned society are often useless for printing in a journal. Those were made for a rapid and superficial examination by an audience when you were talking to them. In print, your illustrations can contain much more detail and must also fit onto the printed page. Most journals will print your illustrations on a half page width in one column to get more on to the page. Thus most pictures need to be in a portrait (longer vertically than horizontally) format rather than in a landscape form. This has a slight advantage in that it emphasises any significant changes in the results plotted on the ordinate.

Next, with some exceptions, most journals do not print illustrations in colour. Photographs of patients and histological preparations are exceptions, but unless the colour is vital you may be asked to pay all or a share of the cost of the colour process. So the

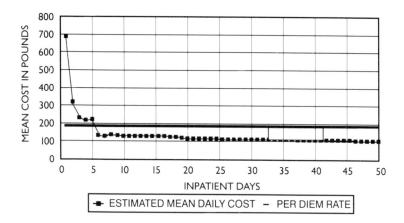

FIGURE I   *Mean cost by patient day (group 2)*

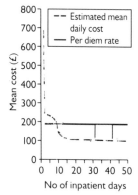

FIGURE I   *Distribution of inpatient costs. Shaded area represents overestimation had per diem costs been used to calculate benefits of reducing length of stay from 42 to 32 days*

Graphs can often be simplified. (Top) figure submitted for publication; (Bottom) as published. Think about the immediate message that needs to come across. The legend should explain the figure completely.

glorious technicolour produced by your favourite computer graphics program will need revision if it is to become a dramatic black and white picture.

Photographs and micrographs

Photographs should include measures to preserve the anonymity of any patient and micrographs should include measures of scale. Both need professional production.

Reproductions of records

If you have a good trace of your experimental results, use it. It will be more effective than a host of words in the text. A trace of the arterial pressure changes accompanying tracheal intubation with and without your therapeutic intervention will make the point rapidly. But take care with the record trace. Firstly, ensure there are calibrations to scale the trace for both pressure and time. Next, talk to staff in your photographic department to make sure the trace is highly visible and if there is a grid it does underlie the trace. Many heat sensitive papers produce a blue trace on a red paper. That is difficult to photograph without the red grid predominating. Use a paper giving a black trace on a green or grey paper. You can get some paper without any background grid. This is acceptable as long as the calibration scales are present. If you are using a photographic paper, such as the ultraviolet light sensitive paper needed for many fast events, talk to staff in your photographic department. They should be able to help you get a black and white trace from a low contrast record. But you will have to take care with the original record and with the reproduction.

Graphics

The bulk of illustrations will be drawings you make to bring out the highlights of your paper. Computer graphics now offer an incredible selection of possibilities. The attraction of three dimensional representation of data as bar graphs, pie charts, or surfaces is almost irresistible. But use these only if there is no other way in which your point can be made. Remember that the eye assesses a three dimensional bar as a volume and not a length. There are a variety of advertisements which should contrast lengths but actually contrast volumes; Tufte's book shows several. Remember to emphasise the data and not the surroundings. The recommendation is to make most of the printer's ink go on the data and to reduce what Tufte calls "the chartjunk." Don't use a full box around the graph if all you need is the abscissa and one ordinate. The best guide will be an examination of the illustrations in the current issues of the journal. Most journals employ professional artists to redraw most of what is submitted—and that costs money.

Finally, for both the illustrations and the tables, remember they must stand alone. Your reader must be able to interpret them without recourse to the text or ideally to other figures and tables. Each table or illustration needs an appropriate legend which explains what is presented. Any abbreviation must be spelt out in full to show its meaning. Each symbol used in a figure must be explained. If you use ± to indicate a standard deviation or error explain which is used. (You don't need to use the ± symbol at all, but you do need to say if the number refers to the deviation or the error.) Draw the reader's attention to any highlight and to the marks for statistical significance. Follow the instruction to authors for your particular journal. Should you have the misfortune to have your paper rejected by one journal, remember to recheck the format needed for the next.

Conclusion

The results section should be the easiest of all to write. You have defined what questions you are going to answer in the design of your study and in the introduction. You have described how you obtained the results in the methods section and shown how accurately you can get the answer. At the design stage you should have ideas as to how you would show the answers. You will have read the instructions to authors. You should know what sorts of record traces you want to show and what sorts of tables and illustrations will be needed. Indeed, apart from filling in the tables and the charts, you could almost write the results section as you start the work. Of course, you will meet the unexpected and you will have to add something extra. But remember that the text will tell the story of what answers you found, the tables will give the meat of the answer, and the illustrations will make the dramatic impressions so the reader will follow you. Keep it straightforward and always consider the reader.

Recommended reading

Chapman M, Mahon B. *Plain figures*. London: HMSO, 1986. (A companion to HMSO's *Plain words*, which is excellent for tables but not so good for figures.)

O'Connor M. *Writing successfully in science*. London: Chapman and Hall, 1991. (A good guide to the whole business.)

Reynolds L, Simmonds D. *Presentation of data in science*. Lancaster: Martinus Nijhoff Publishers, 1984. (A good guide to the preparation of material for talks and for papers for journals.)

Tufte ER. *The visual display of quantitative information*. Cheshire, CT: Graphics Press, 1983. (This book is a tour de force showing what too often is done and what can be done with graphics.)

5 Discussion

ALASTAIR A SPENCE

The discussion section, no less than the other parts of the paper, is an exercise in logic and discipline. It should state the main findings of the study. It should highlight any aspect of the methods that are less than you aimed for (assuming, of course, that this is not a significant confounding factor). You should note previously published findings in the same area of endeavour and, if necessary, try to explain any inconstistency between your work and that of others. Finally, what are the implications of your findings for practice or for future research, or both? These aspects are discussed with the help of imagined examples.

The main findings

> In this study patients who received cyclizine 10 mg intravenously at the end of anaesthesia were half as likely to complain of nausea in the ensuing six hours as those who received intravenous saline (17% v 36%). There was no obvious adverse effect associated with receiving cyclizine.

The two sentences encapsulate the main conclusion of the study without repeating the data, which must be confined to the results section. It is a useful discipline to try to describe the major findings in a sentence or two before starting to write the manuscript. This will be an excellent start to the discussion.

Previous work

> In 1971 Black and White reported no improvement in the incidence of postoperative pulmonary complications associated with the use of a

rebreathing tube. Their assessment, however, was based on x ray changes and oral temperature, which are obviously less specific than the scanning methods we have used. On the other hand, the difference between treatment groups is very similar to that reported by Pink and Blue (1991) in patients recovering from open cholecystectomy: the rebreathing tube had a sparing effect on FRC reduction (21% versus 38% in controls).

Inexperienced authors often write a long and detailed critique about every other paper ever written on the subject. This merely indicates the thoroughness of the literature search; it is necessary to confine your attention to the major players. There are often only a few reputable research groups active in a particular area, and their previous work must be discussed. The judgment of what to put in and what to omit may be difficult; senior colleagues can help with this decision.

Discussion of method

A recognised difficulty in studies of this type is variability in recall of events in the reproductive history (Walker and Jones, 1987). We believe that limiting the period studied to the previous two years is likely to have minimised the source of error.

It is most unlikely that the methods you used in the study were perfect, so you should present a brief appraisal in the discussion. This is particularly important if the design of the study was unusual; you may need to defend vigorously this aspect of the investigation. Hopefully you will have improved on the methods used previously to examine the topic—this is therefore an opportunity to show your work in a good light and even gently chide rivals on the deficits in their work.

What it means for practice

Our findings confirm the value of prophylactic heparin in preventing pelvic vein thrombosis in patients undergoing abdominal hysterectomy. In our large series of 780 patients not a single significant complication of extradural local anaesthetic injection could be found. As a result, the use of heparin in this setting has become part of our hospital practice guidelines.

If your findings may alter clinical practice then this should be discussed. Similarly, if the study was non-clinical, then any basic scientific implications must be mentioned. Most authors are unlikely to make a major breakthrough and it is probable that you have only added another small piece to a large scientific jigsaw. Even so, it is important to state how our scientific understanding has progressed, albeit very little, as a result of your work.

The need for further study?

Although we are much encouraged by the apparent brain protection associated with infusion of omphagon in our rat model, further study of the longer term effects on the brain will be needed before the use of the drug in humans is justified. Also the risk of hepatotoxicity must be defined in view of the occasional finding of hepatocellular injury in these experiments.

A contributor to the *British Journal of Anaesthesia's* guide has observed wryly that the prudent investigator might wish to be well established in the further study before urging the idea on the world at large! This assumes, however, that you will continue in this area of work. If this is unlikely, then you may wish to claim precedence in the discussion for suggesting the next steps in the investigation of the problem.

Some authors like to finish the discussion with a succinct résumé of the major findings. There is a risk of repetition, however, as the same information is likely to have been reported in the abstract (or summary), in the results section, and at the beginning of the discussion. The editor may then simply delete this part of the manuscript in the interests of brevity and clarity. There is a trend away from completing the manuscript in this traditional manner.

Acknowledgements

Acknowledge the source of research funding, and anyone (for example, nurse, technician) whose work, as distinct from attitude of mind, enabled the study to proceed. At the same time, be sure that you should not include them as co-author if they had a unique role. By all means recognise secretaries, wives or husbands, lovers, and parents—but not in the manuscript.

Aims of the discussion
- To state the main findings
- To highlight any shortcomings of the methods
- To compare the results with other published findings
- To discuss the implications of the findings

---

6 Titles, abstract, and authors

J S LILLEYMAN

Richard Asher was, as usual, right. Medical journals *are* dull,[1] and one major contributory factor is the list of long and boring titles. The papers themselves may contain important clinical messages, but the casual reader often doesn't even make the end of the title, let alone the summary. One reason for the problem is that scientific writers are terrified of journalism and, desperately anxious to avoid any hint of sensationalism or hyperbole, veer too far in the direction of tedious obscurity. They also fear the possibility of scientific imprecision creeping in, and the result of these two worries is the long and convoluted titles, perhaps with lengthy subtitles, to be found with depressing frequency in the world's specialist biomedical literature. Asher's fictional example of "A trial of 4, 4-diethyl-hydro-balderdashic acid in acute coryzal infections" (instead of his preferred "A new treatment for colds") is a model of clarity and brevity compared with reality. Glance through a few recent issues of the more rarely thumbed publications in your medical library and you will see what I mean.

Authors seem, on occasion, to be unable to place themselves in the position of their potential readers or, worse, to be indifferent to whether they attract any readers at all. I suppose writers publish scientific papers for a variety of reasons. Their ranks include those who feel it is obligatory for their career but have no relish (as well as no aptitude) for the task, and those who do so purely to satisfy research funding bodies rather than because they have something to tell the world. But because there are so many journals and so few (good) papers, most manuscripts, however boring, confused, or badly written, will eventually appear somewhere. As Asher put it, "every dull dog has his day."

Titles

Whether your article eventually appears in the *Concordian Archives of Postgraduate Research* (a bimonthly publication with 98 subscribers, not listed in *Index Medicus*) or a core journal emblazoned in *Current Contents* with an impact factor of 25 and a worldwide circulation of over 10 000 copies depends, of course, on what it is about and how novel or exciting it is. But it also depends to a greater extent than might be realised on how well written and interestingly presented it is—and the title is an important beginning.

Too few authors realise how much the time spent on this vital part of their creation will be rewarded. When a manuscript arrives on an editor's desk, the title is the first thing that will be seen. It can immediately prejudice the way the paper is handled—whether it is scanned immediately, put to one side, or handed to someone else. When a paper is published, it is the title that the reader sees first in the contents list, and the casual browser might or might not be seduced into turning to the appropriate page. More importantly, the committed reader, a worker in the same field, might miss a relevant paper on "first pass" if the title is elliptical or obscure.

To be fair, there is not much guidance about titles contained in most instructions to authors. The guidelines of the International Committee of Medical Journal Editors (Vancouver Group) do not dwell on the topic beyond indicating that titles should be "concise and informative,"[2] and few journals comment specifically on the matter when describing their house style. One exception is the *New England Journal of Medicine*, which states that "titles should be concise and descriptive (not declarative)." This useful advice means that authors should resist the challenge of trying to condense the whole of their paper into the title—results, conclusions, and all—an exercise attempted surprisingly often.

So how should a title be constructed?

Firstly, and above all else, it should convey, in easily understood terms, what the paper is about. Secondly, it should be as short as possible, and thirdly it should excite rather than stifle interest.

Indicate subject matter

When indicating what the paper is about, do just that. Do not say why it was written, what the findings were, or what conclusions were drawn. Let the reader know the subject matter of the report, not its detailed contents.

Exactly how a title should be worded depends to some extent on the journal to which the article is being submitted. The target readership may be (a) laity, (b) medical workers from outside your own specialty, (c) professionals within your own broad specialty, or (d) the cognoscenti within your own superspecialty. You may reflect this in the use or avoidance of technical words but, generally, a golden rule is—the simpler the better. Trendy jargon should always be avoided. Apart from obscuring meaning, such language often has a short shelf life and dates your publication as effectively as flared jeans.

So, take an imaginary manuscript with the clumsy draft title:

> An epidemiologically-based population-based study of the quantity and effects of background environmental low dose ionising radiation received by male employees of a nuclear reprocessing plant, their first degree relatives, and nearby residents, is indicative of a geographically defined increased risk of germ cell dysfunction and childhood leukaemia in subsequently fathered children.

Remove the conclusion and stick to saying what it is about in simple language: Try instead:

> An epidemiological study of background environmental low dose radiation received by male employees of a nuclear reprocessing plant, their first degree relatives, and nearby residents, and its relation to the local incidence of childhood leukaemia.

But that is still far too long. It needs to be much shorter and more interesting.

Be brief

When Polonius lengthily explained to Gertrude about brevity being the soul of wit, he might usefully have added that it is also vital for successful communication in writing. Short titles tend to be more arresting. They also take up less space, are usually clearer, and are inevitably preferred by editors. It is worthwhile, when you think that the title you have arrived at is as short and pithy as possible, to see how many more words can be squeezed out of it without loss of meaning. It is also quite enjoyable as an intellectual exercise. Definite articles can usually be dispensed with (though that is a matter of style), and excessive adjectives, and "noun salads" (a string of nouns masquerading as adjectives to form clumsy phrases like "community hospital liaison nurse activity analysis") can usually be ruthlessly pruned.

Revisit the leukaemia paper, and now try:

> Environmental radiation near a nuclear reprocessing plant and its relation to local incidence of childhood leukaemia: an epidemiological study.

Be interesting

Finally, do not be afraid of attempting to provoke interest. As Asher put it, an author should try to make the title "allure as well as inform," but be careful never to stray into the world of sensationalism. You are not indulging in the art form of writing headlines and "Leukaemia shock from nuclear waste dump" should be left to the tabloid professionals. Our epidemiology paper already has an arresting title, because the subject matter is politically sensitive as well as clinically important, but if we want to ensure that it has maximum impact for a general readership we might go as far as:

> Nuclear reprocessing, environmental radiation, and childhood leukaemia: an epidemiological study.

This title still confines itself to conveying what the paper is about and is not misleading. It contains all the key words to allow electronic storage and retrieval to be achieved reliably. It is easy to understand, catches the eye, and provokes curiosity. The reader will now have to proceed at least as far as the abstract or summary to learn more. If that happens the title will have served its purpose well.

Guidelines for producing a good title

- The simpler the title the better
- Consider the target readership
- Be brief—short titles are clearer and more arresting
- House style determines whether definite articles are left in
- Avoid excessive adjectives and noun strings
- Do not be sensationalist

Abstracts

The *British Medical Journal* and the *New England Journal of Medicine* call them abstracts, the *Lancet* (at least in its author notes) calls them summaries. In this context the words mean the same. Both refer to a brief statement of the chief points of a larger work.

After the title, the abstract is the second most read part (frequently the only other read part) of a paper, and so is likely to be the basis on which the work is judged by uncritical readers. It is also the first part of a paper that an editor reads carefully, and it may provoke the choice of referees. Like the title, the abstract will reward time spent on it and should be short, intelligible, informative, and interesting. It should be a digest of the whole paper and contain its essence. It should stand alone and will then be helpful to those who, through electronic abstracting services, have access only to the summary and not the whole paper. There will be many such users. There will also be library readers of the whole paper who, for reasons of economy, may copy only the abstract to remind them of the contents. In short, there is every reason to spend a great deal of effort on getting an abstract as near perfect as possible and making it the most highly polished part of the paper.

Despite this, abstracts are often poorly constructed, meandering, and uninformative. Vital bits are left out, or the reader is left hanging at the end as the authors weakly finish by saying that "the findings are discussed"—not much use that is if the main paper is not readily available, and an annoyance that further effort is necessary even if it is. Frustrated editors of some jourals have got so weary of trying to lick indifferent summaries into shape that they have insisted that they be formally structured with labelled headings to make sure that the right bits go in and nothing gets left out.

So, what should an abstract contain? It should consist of four basic parts, which can vary individually in length. These should describe succinctly (a) why what was done was done; (b) what was done; (c) what was found; and (d) what was concluded. The permissible length may be defined by the journal in question, but 200 words is a good average target that should be exceeded only in exceptional circumstances. The Vancouver Group suggests a maximum of 150 words for unstructured abstracts and 250 for fully structured formats.

A worked example

Consider each section of the abstract in turn and write it as a separate paragraph. *Why what was done was done* should contain one or two sentences to orientate the reader and indicate the reason for the study.

> Snibbo is a novel compound for the treatment of reactive depression, but so far only anecdotal reports have indicated that it is effective. We attempted a formal controlled trial in National Health Service (NHS) workers.

What was done should describe, briefly, the methods used.

> A randomised double blind study of consecutively encountered clinically depressed employees from a large NHS district hospital in Greater Gloomsville was undertaken. Snibbo (2 mg/kg/day) was compared with placebo. Participants were assessed at 0, 3, and 6 months by a standardised Cheerup assessment and their socially adjusted misery scores recorded.

What was found should include a synopsis of the results, including the size of the study groups and all basic figures.

> One hundred volunteers were recruited, of whom 48 received Snibbo and 52 placebo. There was no difference in the misery scores at 0 and 3 months, but at 6 months those in the Snibbo group had a range of scores of 2–40 (median 22) compared with 17–82 (median 47) in the other group, showing a difference in median score of 23 (95% confidence interval 15–45; $p < 0.01$).

What can be concluded records what can be learnt from the paper, and should make clear its message to the world.

> For the relief of depression, at least in health service workers, Snibbo appears to be more effective than placebo, but only after it has been taken for more than 3 months.

Structuring an abstract

The *New England Journal of Medicine* would structure the above 160 word abstract by the same four paragraphs and head them Background, Methods, Results, and Conclusions. The *British Medical Journal*'s abstract structure is more detailed and, as well as Objectives, Results, and Conclusions, splits the "what was done" section into Design, Setting, Subjects, and Main Outcome Measures. But the principle is the same, and other journals that use formal structured abstracts all follow a similar basic four part template.

What to leave out

As well as making sure that the right things go into an abstract, it is helpful to be clear about what can be left out. There is no need for a flowery introduction which will be repeated in the appropriate section of the main paper, and there is no need to describe the patients studied in detail, listing each and every exclusion. Results should give adequate details of the main findings (including basic grouped figures, together with statistical confidence intervals and p values) but not what might be called epiphenomena, and conclusions should be clear and uncluttered without discussion drifting about "on the other hand."

Try reading it aloud

When finished, see if the text of the abstract flows by reading it aloud to a colleague unfamiliar with the work. This final test will highlight any remaining ambiguities or obscurities, and will enable the final gloss to be applied. The process takes time. Remember, text that is easy to read is usually hard to write.

Key words

The Vancouver Group guidelines also suggest that up to 10 key words or phrases to assist indexers should be given at the end of abstracts. These should be based on subject matter, and on categories in which you might search for such an article if you were doing a literature trawl yourself. For the above example appropriate key words might include: "antidepressives, depression, Snibbo," and a suitable title for the paper might be "Snibbo for reactive depression: a randomised trial."

Guidelines for producing a good abstract

- The abstract should contain the essence of the whole paper and should stand alone
- It should consist of four basic parts:
  Why the study was done
  What was done
  What was found
  What was concluded
- Stick to a maximum of 150 words for an unstructured abstract and 250 for a structured one
- Be clear and concise and avoid unnecessary detail

Authorship

When considering the question of who should co-author a paper, the Vancouver Group is quite vociferous and restrictive.[2] It says that all authors should have made "substantial" contributions to (a) the concept and design of an experiment, or analysis and interpretation of data; (b) drafting the article or revising it critically for important intellectual content; and (c) final approval of the version to be published: all three, not just one. General supervision of the research group, or just participation in data collection, or simply raising the funds for the project are not considered sufficient.

The Vancouver Group guidelines also suggest that where large collaborative groups are concerned, the key people responsible for the article should be specified, with other contributors being listed separately in an acknowledgement.

This doctrine approaches perfection, and in the real cut and thrust world of biomedical research it must be admitted that sometimes "politically expedient" authors do creep on to the list. Indeed, inclusion of heads of departments at the end of author lists is regarded by some groups as a convention, and perhaps has a small advantage in that it may indicate that the work comes from a pedigree unit. Or otherwise. But purists would argue that this is irrelevant, that referees should read papers "blind" (very hard in practice, even if the title page is removed), and that submitted work should be assessed purely on its intrinsic merits. They would insist that the Vancouver guidelines for authors should be followed ruthlessly.

It is important that all authors should sign a submission letter or a note of agreement to include them as authors. There have been instances of fraud where names have been taken in vain, and most editors are now wary of the fact.

It is in the interest of authors to keep their numbers small if they like to see their names in reference lists and in indexing and abstracting services. The ideal number is one or two; then both names are always quoted. With three or more, those not in pole position run an increasing risk of being consigned to *et al*. With more than six, those ranked seven or more may appear in print only in the original article.

So, if possible, keep the numbers down. Ask yourself if Dr Morbid, who did some special histological stains on your case of Snibbo's disease, really needs to be a co-author, or whether he was just doing his job and could be satisfied with a courteous acknowledgement as a footnote. The same might apply to the radiologist who carried out some extracurricular postmortem radiology. Understand that researchers or secretaries who type references into databases or manuscripts love short author lists and detest the task of transcribing endless names. They also love short titles, which brings us back to the beginning.

[1] Asher R. *A sense of Asher: a new miscellany.* London: British Medical Association, 1984.
[2] International Committee of Medical Journal Editors. Uniform requirements for manuscripts submitted to biomedical journals. *BMJ* 1991; **302**: 338–41.

Care for your readers, your editors, and yourself

Remember the following points:
- Provide short and interesting titles
- Painstakingly construct concise, readable, and informative abstracts
- Share the credit with as few people as possible

---

7 References

M J HALSEY

This chapter outlines the techniques for finding the appropriate references for a paper and subsequently presenting them correctly in the manuscript to be submitted for publication. One of the characteristics and strengths of all scientific research is that each investigation has as its foundation the work of predecessors in the field. Thus, knowledge of the published work is critical to the success and soundness of the study, as well as to the credibility of the paper.

Most people will already be aware of some of the publications on their topic. The practical questions are whether they have the key references; whether the references they propose to include in the paper are the right balance between being comprehensive and being relevant; and finally whether there are any new current references about which they ought to be aware.

Initial literature search

It is a cliché to bemoan the expansion of the medical literature, but the important aspect to remember is that it is all organised and systematically indexed. If you understand the basic systems it is relatively easy to gain an entry into the published work. The most widely used index system is *Index Medicus*, an index to periodical articles in the medical sciences covered by the (American) National Library of Medicine. This index is produced in monthly issues which are subsequently combined to produce a cumulative index for the year. The associated computer bibliographic database is Medline. Both indexes are international in scope and cover approximately 75%

of the citations published in the English language; more than 3200 journals are indexed and every article is classified by subject and author.

Classification by subject

Classification by subject is far more sophisticated than simply recording the authors and the title of the article. When an article is indexed for *Index Medicus* or Medline, the indexer at the National Library of Medicine assigns several (on average ten) single or multiterm terms for the most specific topics covered in the article. These medical subject headings (MeSH) are used to cover the central aspects of each article, as well as other significant information discussed in the article. On the other hand, ideas only mentioned in passing will not be indexed. The obvious advantage of this system is that it does not rely on the accuracy and completeness of the title or key words chosen by the original authors.

It is important to understand the ways these MeSH terms are structured. In general the terms that are chosen for the index are as specific as possible. If the researcher searches the literature using a more general term, articles indexed under narrower subterms will not be found. This problem can be overcome in the printed version of *Index Medicus* by first consulting the list of MeSH terms and choosing the most appropriate one for a particular search. In the computer form of the index, Medline, there is a facility for "exploding" a term—that is, the system searches for the selected term plus all its narrower, more specific terms. With this technique you can find information that may not be indexed to the selected term but, because it is indexed to a narrower term, is pertinent to your topic.

It is also possible to limit the numbers of articles being found by including a subheading that describes a specific aspect of the topic (for example, Adverse Effects, Diagnosis, or Pharmacokinetics). If you "explode" a single term, the subheadings are applied to each narrower term as well as to the term itself.

Limitations of the system

There are some limitations to the system which should be remembered. Firstly, it is important to recognise that some key terms may have synonyms and variants as well as English or American spelling; these aspects can usually be overcome by use of the thesaurus facility. Secondly, it should be noted that acronyms are not usually indexed. For example, those searching for articles on AIDS would retrieve articles on financial aids, etc, but not acquired immunodeficiency syndrome (which requires the full and specific spelling). Thirdly, if you are searching back into the literature it must be remembered that there are historical changes in the index terms and even in the journals covered by the system; what may be a suitable search pattern for the current year is not necessarily going to reveal the appropriate articles from 1990.

A general suggestion for checking the adequacy of the search strategy is to be aware of at least a couple of articles that should be retrieved and to check that they do show up. Alternatively, it is possible to check the MeSH headings used for the known articles and then apply these as part of the wider search.

Search systems

The computer based systems subdivide into those that operate on line or via PCs or CD-ROMs: on line search services include Medline, Dialog, PaperChase, and BRS. PC based systems include Current Contents on diskette and Reference Update. The CD-ROM systems include Compact Cambridge and SilverPlatter.

The great advantage of a number of these systems (such as SilverPlatter) is that in addition to the title, author, and MeSH terms the abstract is also available. This enables the researcher to decide quickly if the particular article is relevant or only peripheral to the specific aspect of the topic under consideration. Inevitably such systems are not cheap and have been possible only because of the increased storage capacity provided, for example, by CD-ROMs. However, more medical libraries now have one or other of the systems available, and this approach to literature searching is so much more efficient than manual alternatives.

Alternative indexes

Although *Index Medicus,* with Medline, has become the most widely used index systems in medical research, it should not be forgotten that there are other indexes which serve specific needs.

(1) *Excerpta Medica* is subdivided into clinical specialities and has the advantage of providing a printed abstract (sometimes the authors' and sometimes prepared by a compiler who is an expert in the field). The subjects are subdivided into specific headings and provide a means of keeping up with a specific field of interest within a discipline. In general the journals indexed are confined to clinical medicine and this should be borne in mind when reviewing a specific topic.

(2) *Biological Abstracts* is an example of one of the other indexes which, in this case, concentrates on experimental medicine and the

44

biological sciences. Another example is *Chemical Abstracts,* which dates from 1907 and was one of the original abstracting indexes.

(3) *Science Citation Index* is a system which lists where a particular paper has been cited. It is very useful if a key reference is known and you want to know who has subsequently written on that topic. It is particularly appropriate when the terminology has not yet been included in the MeSH headings of *Index Medicus* and so the more conventional approaches to literature searching are not very efficient. One of the limitations is that it is based on only the first author of the article.

(4) *Five years' cumulative indexes*—Many specialist journals produce cumulative indexes of articles that they have published. This is a reasonable method of initiating a search into the literature, but it is important to know the index terms and subheadings used by any particular journal. Some specialities have standardised their index systems within the discipline, but there are inevitably some idiosyncrasies.

List of printed indexes

- *Index Medicus*
- *Excerpta Medica*
- *Biological Abstracts, Chemical Abstracts,* etc
- *Science Citation Index*
- Journals' cumulative indexes

List of computer databases

There are well over 700 in addition to Medline; examples of the larger ones include:

- Biosis—biology, including clinical and experimental medicine, immunology, pharmacology, biophysics, and biochemistry
- EMBASE (Excerpta Medica)—excludes nursing, veterinary medicine, and dentistry, but is particularly strong on drug related literature
- Health—non-clinical, administration
- IPA—drug development
- Toxline—toxicology, including teratogens, mutagens, carcinogens, pollutants, and pesticides; adverse drug reactions

---

Continuing literature awareness

There is a strong negative correlation between time since graduation and currency of knowledge. This may or may not be true for a particular individual, but all would acknowledge that it requires a conscious effort to keep up to date. This activity goes far beyond reading relevant publications and attending meetings. It is vital that articles can be remembered, that the citations are accurate, and, most important, that the previous work is quoted accurately. Several approaches help in this process.

Regularly reading one or more specialist journals should provide a significant yield of high quality articles directly relevant to your own interests and clinical practice. Many members of departments also meet in one of the many forms of "circulation club" which keep people abreast of a wider field within their discipline.

Review articles now form nearly 5% of the total scientific literature. Those appearing in specialist journals are usually written by accepted authorities in the field. They are not necessarily current because of the inevitable delays in the publication process, but this can be easily checked from the dates in the reference list. Some reviews (such as *Physiological and Pharmacological Reviews*) are not only written by accepted authorities but are also peer reviewed before acceptance for publication. This means that they are a carefully considered assessment of the current position in the field and can be regarded as milestones in the literature. Another type is the *Annual Review* series (of medicine, pharmacology, or physiology) or the *Recent Advances* series (in anaesthesia, etc). Some reviews are not necessarily as authoritative as others, and the fact that a contribution is labelled as a review should not be taken as a seal of academic approval. There has been a proliferation of this type of derivative literature. Those who write reviews know that they are incredibly popular for reprint requests. Finally, it should be noted that there are now reviews of reviews and *Index Medicus* provides annually a special bibliography of medical reviews annually.

Conference proceedings have proved to be a useful source of current material. These are now indexed separately under the title *Proceedings in Print*. It should not be forgotten that often it is the conference itself that provides the peer review and as such the abstracts or precirculated papers may not be as authoritative as they appear. Theses are more carefully considered and are an underutilised source of current thinking in a particular field. The difficulty is access, but this has been helped by the publication of *The Index of Theses accepted for Higher Degrees* and *Dissertation Abstracts International.*

Current Contents provides simple lists of the contents pages of journals and is now available in weekly booklet or PC disk format.

Some commercial companies provide these on a limited scale for journals in a particular discipline as a complementary service to the profession. The whole approach has become less cumbersome with the arrival of computer searching programs. These are based on the words in the titles and, as with Medline, combining a series of specific title words in a search pattern can be very effective in identifying key articles.

Storage of references

Once you have acquired and read the relevant papers carefully, it is vital to make a note of the important information in them and to store the references so that they can be retrieved easily. The traditional method of doing this is on record cards, but it should be noted that if you are going to be doing serious research for, say, three years you could easily accumulate over a thousand references, and a manual system quickly becomes very unwieldy. It is for this reason that people use a computer storage and retrieval system.

There are now several personal reference management systems for use on PCs which are designed to record article citations and to help in the generation of bibliographies for papers. The literature references are entered either by using the keyboard or by linking to one of the search services. It is possible to enter notes or text of any length for each article (subject of course to your computer's storage capacity, which is surprisingly finite in this context). Once the references are entered, you can retrieve them by almost anything you can remember about them (author, keyword, title word or phrase, note, etc).

A major virtue of these programs is that they can generate bibliographies formated in virtually any journal style and can incorporate the appropriate reference citations into a manuscript. It is not just a question of making life easier. Using a computer generated reference section does ensure that the original references need be checked only at the time of entry, and the subsequent generation of drafts and revisions does not result in inaccuracies creeping into the pristine reference section.

A leading computer system in this area is Reference Manager. It was first developed in 1972 and many quirks have since been ironed out. It has the advantage that the program and a copy of the main database can be installed on as many computers as you wish. The only restriction is that the same database must be copied to each computer. Anyone purchasing for the first time should inquire about what and when will be the next update version and what will be its advantages.

Producing the reference section in a paper

Except for review articles, long lists of references are usually inappropriate. Restrict references to those that have a direct bearing on the work described. As a guide, it is rarely necessary to cite more than forty works for the longest of papers. In general cite only references to books listed in *Books in Print* or to articles published in journals indexed by *Index Medicus*.

There are two major methods of referring to the bibliographic material: the Vancouver system, which is becoming widely preferred,[1] and the Harvard system, which is retained by a few journals. Even if you know which system is used by the particular journal to which you wish to submit a paper, check the specific guide to contributors as well, because there are still many minor variations in the layout.

Don't regard the reference section of the paper as a minor chore to be left to the last moment or to the most junior author (or the secretary typing the paper). Submission of references that are inappropriate, inaccurate, or in the wrong format may appear to the inexperienced author to be only a technical issue, but to an editor it may be sufficient reason for returning the paper for retyping before even considering it. If it gets past the editorial office it is not unknown for assessors to recognise that the references are in the style of another journal and to conclude that the paper has already been rejected for publication at least once, and to scrutinise the whole article more harshly.

Word processors enable reference lists to be corrected and amended, but the fact that a reference looks right is dangerously deceptive. There is a tried and tested way of finally checking the reference list; photocopy the first page of every reference cited; at the same time, make sure that this page includes all the details commonly needed in reference lists whatever the preferred format (for example last page numbers, book publisher's name and location). Keep these first pages with the hard copy of the evolving manuscript and use them to check directly both the final submitted version and the proof copy.

Guidelines for producing a useful reference list

- Restrict the list to those references with a direct bearing on the work described
- For references to journal articles cite only references to journals listed in *Index Medicus*
- Check the house style on whether the Vancouver or Harvard system is used
- Check the instructions to authors and make sure that you have included all of the necessary details for each reference

---

The Vancouver system

References are numbered consecutively in the order in which they are first mentioned in the text. References in text, tables, and legends are identified by arabic numbers appearing in the text either in brackets (usually specified as square, but not by all journals) or as superscripts. The alternative variation on this, used for some review articles in journals otherwise conforming to the Vancouver system, is for the references to be arranged alphabetically in the reference list and numbered accordingly in both list and text.

Sometimes authors consider it essential to cite the names of authors of a study in the text (in addition to the identifying number). Here the convention is to cite only up to three names (Adams, Smith and Jones [24] have shown . . .). If there are more than three names it is better to use a phrase such as "Birt and colleagues [25]" or "Hall and co-workers [26]." The expression *"et al"* is not encouraged by most editors. Sometimes people use an informal reference to previous work (Nunn's study; or Mushin's work) but in this case the paragraph must always contain the reference cited formally as well; this is usually at the end of the specific sentence.

The Harvard system

In this system the order of references at the end of the paper is strictly alphabetical, regardless of chronology. The style of citations varies slightly from journal to journal. In the text, references should be made by giving in parentheses the name of the author and the year of publication—for example, (Hall, 1988)— except where the author's name is part of the sentence—for example, Hall (1988) showed that . . . ." Where several references are given together they should be listed in chronological order and separated by semicolons. When a paper written by two authors is quoted, both names are given; if there are more than two authors all the names should be given the first time the reference is cited, but after that it is sufficient to give the first name only, adding *et al.* When two citations have same author(s) and the same year of publication, alphabetical annotation is used—for example, (Nunn, 1991a) and (Nunn, 1991b). The order of alphabetically annotated citations should ideally be chronological within the year, but this is the counsel of perfection.

Guidelines common to both systems

Text references to "unpublished observations" or "personal communications" should not be included in the final list of references. "Unpublished observations" include information from manuscripts submitted but not yet accepted for publication; don't try to slip in another piece of work by including it in the reference list as "submitted for publication." If the other work is critically important to the present paper wait until the former has been accepted for publication before submitting the present manuscript. "Personal communications" should be cited in the text as: [Brown AB, personal communication]. The authors have responsibility for ensuring that the exact wording of references to unpublished work is both seen and approved by the person concerned.

Papers that have been submitted and accepted for publication should be included in the list, the phrase "in press" replacing volume and page number. Authors should be prepared to give the volume and page number at the time of proof correction.

Format for the reference list

The list of references at the conclusion of the paper begins on a new sheet of paper. The easiest way of ensuring that you have the right format for this part is to look both at the journal's instructions to authors and at a couple of reference lists in current papers in the same journal. If in doubt the usual convention is as follows:

Journal article—Surname and initials of all authors (not *et al*, however many authors), full title of paper, full title of journal (with capitalisation of both nouns and adjectives), year of publication, volume number (not issue number unless it is a supplement), first and last pages of article. Some parts of journals have letters following or preceding the page numbers (for example, P (for Proceedings), A (for Abstract), S (for Supplement)). If such designation letters are used they should always be included in the reference citation of the pages.

Book or monograph—Surname and initials of author(s), full title of book (usually underlined), number of edition, town of publication, publisher, year of publication. In general it is desirable to be as specific as possible in a book reference so add specific pages to the quotation if they are relevant but don't make the citation too complex or repetitive.

Chapter in a multi-author book—Chapter author, initials, chapter title, book authors (or editors), and initials, book title, town of publication, publisher, year of publication, first and last pages.

Proceedings of conferences—Only include these if the proceedings have been published in an *Index Medicus* journal or in a recognised book; in the former case use the journal format (with a designation letter if included); in the latter case use the book chapter format (with the designation "Proceedings of . . ." if it appears in the book title).

Conclusion

The importance of the reference section of a paper is sometimes underestimated by inexperienced authors. In fact it is critical to the credibility of the paper. In 1985 an analysis of the quotations and references in medical journals revealed serious deficiencies.[2] It was discovered that 20% of the references appearing in the *British Medical Journal* were misquoted, with half of these misquotations being seriously misleading. In the *British Journal of Surgery* as many as 46% of all citations were wrong, with 39% of these errors being major (that is, the article could not be located).

Since that time editors, assessors, and reviewers have been determined to improve the situation. Inaccurate quotations and citations are displeasing for the original author and misleading for the reader, and mean that untruths become "accepted fact." Current authors should be aware that if their reference sections are not of the highest standard, it is they who will be castigated by future generations of researchers attempting to search the literature.

[1] International Committee of Medical Journal Editors. Uniform requirements for manuscripts submitted to biomedical journals. *BMJ* 1991; **302**: 338–41.
[2] De Lacey G, Record C, Wade J. How accurate are quotations and references in medical journals. *BMJ* 1985; **291**: 884–6.

8 How to write a letter

General considerations

When wishing to submit a letter to a journal first consider the following basic questions:

- What is the purpose of your letter?
- Is a letter format appropriate for this particular journal?
- Does what you want to say justify a communication?

The purpose of a letter varies between journals (box 1). Most letters are comments in response to a previous publication, though brief communications that do not justify a full report are sometimes appropriate as letters. It is always wise to read the instructions for authors and to examine the correspondence section of recent issues of the journal to gain a feel for the style and scope of successful (that

---

BOX 1: The purpose of a letter

Usual:
Comment against or in favour of a previous publication
Communication of case report(s)
Concise communication of clinical or investigative data

Less common:
General medical or political comment (for example, "guild issues")
Comment concerning the nature or format of the journal
Advertisement of interest to collaborate or gain access to patients or study material

---

is, published!) letters. Always question whether the information you wish to convey truly justifies publication—minor comments or observations are unlikely to be accepted.

If the purpose and content of your communication seem appropriate for the letter format two other major considerations are the length of the letter and the style of presentation. With respect to length, always be brief. All journal editors like concise communications. They would rather publish ten short letters on ten different topics than two lengthy ones on only two topics. Think what it is like yourself as a reader—messages are always more effective if put briefly. Some journals impose firm restrictions on length and number of accompanying tables or figures. This will be in the instructions to authors, but even if it is not overtly stated all editors favour a Raymond Chandler over a Charles Dickens. For example, compare the following two extracts.

Sir,

I feel I must put pen to paper with respect to the recent communication by Dr Peter Jones and colleagues in your August issue[1] to draw the attention of your readers to possible misinterpretation of the data presented. Although these excellent workers have a proven track record in the field of complement activation (not only in rheumatoid arthritis but in other inflammatory diseases as well), in this present study they appear to have omitted to properly control for varying degrees of inflammation in the knee joints of the patients that they aspirated—not only those with rheumatoid arthritis but also those with osteoarthritis. Such inflammation of the knee joint could have been assessed either by local examination and scoring for features such as temperature increase, effusion, synovial thickening, anterior joint line tenderness, duration of early morning stiffness, and duration of inactivity stiffness, with addition of the different scores to a single numerical value (that is, the system devised and tested by Robin Cooke and colleagues in Alberta[2]) and/or by simultaneous measurement and comparison to levels of other markers of inflammation, for example the synovial fluid total white cell and differential (particularly polymorphonuclear cell) count, or local synovial fluid levels of various arachidonic acid products such as prostaglandins or leukotrienes.

(Dr C Dickens)

Sir,

In their study of synovial fluid complement activation Jones *et al*[1] made no assessment of the inflammatory state of aspirated knees. Such assessment could have been attempted using the summated six point clinical scoring system of Cooke *et al*[2] or by estimation of alternative indicators of inflammation (for example, cell counts, prostaglandins, leukotrienes). (Dr R Chandler)

Both convey the same message. The second, however, is more "punchy" and gets straight to the point by omitting unnecessary description and detail. As with any scientific writing, try to keep sentences short. Make each of your points separately. Reference short statements rather than provide extended summaries of previous work.

Etiquette and style for letters in response to an article

A letter is the accepted format for comment relating to a previous publication in the same journal. Occasionally it may relate to a publication in another journal.

The usual purpose of such a letter is to offer support or criticism (most commonly criticism) of the rationale, method, analysis, or conclusion of the previous study. If this is the case make specific, reasoned criticisms or provide additional pertinent data to be considered in the topic under consideration. Do not reiterate arguments already fully covered or referenced in the provoking publication. Your letter should raise points not adequately addressed or provide information that additionally supports the contentions of the other authors. However prestigious you may think yourself, merely offering your personal dissent or approval is not enough. You should use the letter to argue a reasoned perspective. It should not be a vehicle for biased opinion. Always be specific. General comments unsubstantiated by reasoned argument ("I think this a great publication," "I think it's rubbish") are unacceptable.

If offering criticism always be courteous, never rude, arrogant, or condescending. Apart from common decency to fellow investigators, politeness in correspondence will serve to enhance and safeguard whatever reputation you have. This is the same golden rule that applies to question time at oral presentations. No one likes a rude critic, even (or more especially) one who is right. A polite, understated question or comment inevitably has more critical impact than arrogant dismissal. For example, compare the following two styles of presentation. Both letters make the same points.

Sir,
I was greatly surprised that the paper on synovial fluid complement breakdown products (C3dg) by Jones *et al*[1] managed to get into your

journal. Firstly, Jones *et al* obviously forgot to control for the inflammatory state of the knees that they aspirated, even though we have previously drawn attention to the importance of this in any synovial fluid study.[2] Secondly, they made no attempt to determine levels of C3dg in synovial fluid from normal knees. Since they only compared findings between rheumatoid and pyrophosphate arthritis knees it is hardly surprising that they jump to the wrong conclusion in stating that complement activation is not a prominent feature of pyrophosphate arthropathy. Thirdly, they only reported C3dg concentrations with no correction for synovial fluid native C3 levels. If these investigators had only taken the time to read the existing literature they would have realised that we previously have shown that such correction is of paramount importance for correct interpretation of C3dg data. That such a majorly flawed paper, which does not even reference our seminal work,[2] should be published at all, let alone as an extended paper, must seriously question the effectiveness of the peer review system that you operate.

A Pratt

Sir,

I was interested in the study of synovial fluid breakdown products (C3dg) by Jones *et al*[1] in which they conclude, contrary to our previous report,[2] that complement activation is not a feature of chronic pyrophosphate arthropathy. The discordance between these studies is most likely to relate to differences in clinical characterisation and expression of C3dg levels rather than to estimation of C3dg itself. Unlike Jones *et al* we assessed and controlled for the inflammatory state of aspirated knees; included normal knees as a control group; and corrected for native C3 concentrations (expressed as a ratio C3dg/C3), as well as reporting C3dg concentrations. Employing these methods, we were able to demonstrate complement activation in clinically inflamed, but not quiescent, pyrophosphate arthritis knees. Such activation was quantitatvely less marked than that observed in active rheumatoid knees. We would suggest that clinical assessment of inflammatory state, inclusion of normal knee controls, and correction for native C3 levels be considered in future synovial fluid studies.

A Diplomat

Remember that in almost all journals the original authors will be given the chance to respond to your criticisms. It is much easier to respond to a rude than a polite letter, and even potentially damning points that you raise may get lost in the "noise" of confrontation. For example, in reply to Dr Pratt's letter Dr Jones would be able to centre his reply around defence of the peer review system. However, he would be hard pressed to sidestep the same specific criticisms levelled by Dr Diplomat. Furthermore, the original authors have the last word and if your criticisms are misplaced (it happens!) you will not be able to rescind and may find yourself publicly ridiculed, appearing as a rude ignoramus rather than an interested and inquiring intellectual. For example:

> Sir,
> We are grateful to Dr Pratt for his comments. We had in fact carefully considered all the points he raises. Because all knees included in our study were clinically inflamed the question of correcting for differing degrees of inflammation does not arise. We also considered aspiration of normal knees but this was not approved by our local ethics committee. We included estimation of native C3 and expression of C3dg/C3 in our original manuscript. This made no difference to the results and because the main thrust of our paper dealt with the method, not the demonstration, of C3 activation in rheumatoid knees (with original data on C4d and factor B activation) we were asked to delete these data by the expert reviewers. We were of course aware of the study by Dr Pratt and colleagues but were limited in the number of references we could include. We therefore referred to the first report of synovial fluid C3dg in normal, rheumatoid and pyrophosphate arthritis knees by Earnest *et al*[1] which predated that of Pratt *et al* by six years.

Note that letters are always directed to the editor, never to the initial author. The editor in this situation is an impartial intermediary between authors, particularly those in potential conflict.

BOX 2: Guidelines for a letter in response to an article

- Be courteous and interested, not rude or dismissive
- Make specific rather than general comments
- Give reasoned argument, not biased opinion
- Do not repeat aspects already covered in the original article
- Introduce a different perspective or additional data to the topic
- Attempt to make only one or a very few specific points
- Be concise

Other forms of letter

In many journals the correspondence section is an appropriate site for short reports with a simple message that do not necessitate a full paper. This is particularly true if a study uses standard techniques that are readily referenced and require no detailed explanation.

Presentation of a study as a letter is rather similar to writing an extended abstract (box 3). There should normally be three clear divisions: an introduction relating the rationale and objectives of the study, a section stating the methods and results, and, finally, a conclusion which assesses the validity and importance of the findings in the context of other work. Unlike in concise or extended papers, section headings are not used and an abstract is unnecessary.

BOX 3: Presentation of a concise report as a letter

- Introduce the topic:
  Briefly explain rationale and objectives of study
- Present methods and results:
  Reference methods as much as possible
  Include only essential data
  Tabulate results if possible
- Present conclusions:
  Emphasise only one or a few major conclusions
  Avoid extrapolating too far from data
- Avoid repetition of data or conclusions
- Be concise

Although often considered a "second rate" way of reporting data, a letter format is quite appropriate for brief reports and can still be prestigious (particularly in certain journals). If presenting original data in a letter consider carefully whether this will compromise any aspiration to subsequently publish the same data in a more extended form. Remember that letters can be referenced and that dual publication must be avoided.

Case reports are often presented as letters. This is particularly suitable for single cases that do not justify a full or concise report. Some journals have no specific slot for case reports and publish all cases as letters. Most editors will expect to receive only cases that give novel insight into pathogenesis, diagnosis, or management. As with short reports, cases are best divided into a brief introduction, description of the case itself, and then discussion of its interest, with no section headings. Be particularly careful not to repeat the same information by summarising the case at the beginning and the end (a common mistake and easy to do).

General or political comment mainly occurs in general journals or specialist journals that are the official outlet of learned societies. In this situation humorous comments may be permitted (though they are somewhat risky). Letters may be used to advertise an interest in particular cases or investigational material for research purposes, or of a service on offer (for example, DNA repository). Such advertisements should be very brief and are more usually found in a notes/news section.

9 How to write an abstract for a scientific meeting

R N Allan

It is, of course, preposterous, impossible, insulting, and unacceptable that anyone should insist that your work, which has consumed your every waking moment for at least the past twelve months and which quite clearly is at the forefront of scientific developments, should be reduced to 200 words. Take a few slow, deep breaths, recover your equilibrium, and pause for thought, perhaps even mustering a little sympathy for the society organising the meeting at which you wish to present your original scientific work.

The scientific meeting and the programme will have been planned several years in advance. The lectures and symposia will have been agreed, the national and international speakers invited, and the venue selected. In addition, the scientific programme will include a limited number of spaces for presentation of abstracts, either as oral communications or posters.

Selection of abstracts

Since the number of abstracts usually exceeds the number of spaces, some sort of selection procedure must be introduced. A large panel of reviewers, experts in their own fields, is usually selected to read and mark each abstract. Each reviewer usually has many abstracts to assess, so the time allocated to read your own precious abstract may well be short. Furthermore, the secretariat organising the meeting will know that authors commonly ignore instructions and usually submit abstracts over length, illegible, incomplete, and late. They will be determined on this occasion to ensure that only

59

abstracts which conform completely to the guidelines will be considered. Be warned!

Guidelines

The instructions may look (and usually are) tedious, but they are designed to ensure high quality reproduction of your work. Until recently, accepted abstracts were edited and then typeset so that well presented abstracts were published, regardless of the quality of the original submission. For speed and efficiency most abstracts are now photographed and reproduced exactly as they appeared when submitted (camera ready abstracts). The abstract must be typed within the prescribed area. The appropriately sized typeface and a high quality, preferably a laser, printer should be used to ensure good reproduction. Direct reproduction of the camera ready abstract will mean that any errors in spelling, grammar, or scientific fact will be reproduced exactly as you have typed them—so take care. Vain hopes that the photographic process might in some way enhance your abstract must be abandoned at an early stage.

Send the appropriate number of copies. Anonymous copies, without the names of the author and the institution where the work was carried out, are often requested to ensure that the marking process is independent and fair. Make a careful note of the deadline; preparation of abstracts always takes longer than expected. Late entries, or those not conforming to the guidelines, may be rejected out of hand without evaluation.

The abstract form commonly includes a number of categories, and the most appropriate category for your work must be selected and marked to ensure that the selected reviewer is an expert in your field. You must decide whether the abstract should be considered for a poster only, an oral presentation, or either. You will often be invited to declare that the abstract is completely original, and if the abstract has been submitted to another meeting or for publication the full details must be given in a covering letter.

Preparation of the abstract

It is helpful to prepare the abstract using a number of headings, even though the headings themselves may eventually be deleted from the final text.

Title

The title is a concise summary of the abstract and must encourage the assessors to believe that the work is important, relevant, and innovative. Write out the key features of your work and string them together in half a dozen words until the title effectively conveys the message.

Authors

Include authors who have really contributed to the work. It is assumed, if the abstract is accepted, that the first author will present the work. The author presenting the work often has to be identified. The name and address of the institution where the majority of the work was carried out is usually included, as is the telephone number where the authors can be reached should problems arise. For example, your abstract may be selected for a plenary session; then the organisers will need to confirm that the presenter speaks fluent English and that the authors agree that the work is sufficiently important for such a session.

Background

A sentence or two summarising previous work relevant to the presentation is important. Highlight any controversies which your work has helped to resolve.

Aims

What is the point of the study? What is the hypothesis? How is it different from previous work? Is it useful, exciting, and worthwhile, and does it contribute significantly in the area? Encapsulating these ideas in a sentence or two takes practice.

Patients

If patients were studied, how were they selected? Did they give informed consent; was the selection of patients random; why were patients excluded?

Methods

The techniques employed must be summarised and novel methods described in greater detail. Minimise the use of abbreviations, which only confuse the reviewer and colleagues. Note the methods used to test for statistical significance.

61

Results

Patient data should be provided first, including numbers studied, sex, age distribution, and duration of follow up. The key results should then be summarised, usually in four or five sentences identifying the positive features, ensuring that any claims made can be substantiated in the presentation or discussion. Highlight new developments.

Discussion

What has the work added to the existing body of knowledge? In what way are these new findings important? Could the findings have occurred by chance, or are they statistically significant?

Conclusions and implications

Why is the work important? What are the next steps to develop the work further?

From draft to final version

The draft outline of the abstract is now complete. It will probably be hopelessly over length. Producing the same information in an abstract of less than 200 words must be seen as an exciting challenge. Delete any duplicate information; delete superfluous or irrelevant information. Can the same idea be conveyed in fewer words? If the abstract is still over length, what are the most important features in the results? Can some of the results be omitted and presented at the meeting?

It will take time and many drafts to produce the desired outcome; start early and plan to have the abstract completed and submitted well before the deadline. The abstract must primarily reflect the work that has been carried out, but do not forget that it must also be attractive to the reviewers and catch their eye in that "brief moment of time" as your abstract is assessed.

Recheck the guidelines and ensure that you and the typist have conformed in all respects with the instructions. Photocopy the original abstract form and ensure that the draft abstract can be laid out effectively within the space available. Circulate the draft abstract to your colleagues and obtain their approval for submission.

Final typing

Only then can the final typing be completed, the appropriate number of named and anonymous copies obtained, and the abstract submitted. Do not duplicate results—two or more abstracts describing similar results of one study are both likely to be rejected. You may need to include a self addressed envelope in order to learn the outcome of the assessor's evaluation.

Outcome

In due course, you will hear the outcome of the assessment and experience the joy of acceptance or the depression of rejection. Few abstracts are outstanding and few are awful. The marks for most abstracts hover around the mean and are either just accepted or just rejected. Temper the joy of acceptance with modesty; the depression of rejection can be minimised by the knowledge that the abstract was probably only just rejected. Resubmission with minor modifications to the next meeting will probably be successful.

Presenting the data

Writing an abstract is only the first phase. The accepted abstract has to be converted into an oral presentation or a poster—another exciting challenge. Submission of an abstract implies that one of the authors will present the paper or poster in person at the meeting. Late withdrawal of an abstract gives the individual and the unit a bad name.

Conclusion

An abstract that summarises your work clearly and concisely and has an apparently effortless presentation can be achieved only with meticulous preparation, but in doing so you will sense the excitement and achievement of contributing at the forefront of new scientific developments.

10 How to write a case report

J A W WILDSMITH

Case reporting is arguably the oldest and most basic form of communication in medicine. The verbal presentation and explanation of a case history is a skill that is acquired early in undergraduate training and is one that most clinicians use throughout their careers. Much the same ability is required in making a written presentation: the positive features have to be detailed in a sequential and logical fashion, together with that "negative" material that is directly relevant. A case report is, for many clinicians, the first entry into print and, because the basic methodology is familiar, it is a useful exercise in learning to write.

That point made, it is important to remember that all the rules defining other forms of medical writing apply equally to the case report. Clear, unambiguous English should be used to present the material so that the reader has a clear understanding of:

- what happened to the patient
- the time course of these events
- why management followed the lines that it did.

The key feature of a good case report is that it should help the reader to recognise and deal with a similar problem should one ever present itself.

In preparing a case report the writer should be asking three questions: What am I going to report? How should I report it? In which journal shall I aim to publish the report?

What to report

Few doctors do not occasionally come across a patient whose condition might merit production of a case report. The key is to both observe and think about clinical practice. In today's circumstances it is a very lucky doctor who describes a totally original condition, but there are many rare or unusual patients who may merit description. However, rarity is not, in itself, cause for publication. The case must be special and have a "message" for the reader. It could be to raise awareness of the condition so that the diagnosis may be made more readily in the future, or the report might indicate how one line of treatment was more suitable and effective than another. What such case reports do, to draw a legal parallel, is establish "case law" for relatively rare disease states.

The second group of patients who may be worth reporting are those with unusual, perhaps even unknown, conjunctions of conditions which may have opposing priorities in their managements. A variation on this theme is the patient who presents with a rare or unusual complication of a disease or therapeutic procedure. Again, though, it is important to indicate what message there is in *this* patient's case for those who read about it. Almost as important as the message is that the case should be interesting to read about. Clearly, skill as an author is going to influence readability, but no amount of writing skill is going to make an uneventful case interesting.

It is as well to remember from the beginning that the first reader of the report will be the editor. Although some editors are totally averse, many feel that case reports help to attract readers by making their journals seem a little more relevant to "ordinary" clinicians who consider that the more scientific contributions do not immediately interest them. Most editors whose journals include case reports receive many more than they have space to publish, so it is up to the writer to ensure that the report is unusual, interesting, and readable so that it is accepted.

Assess the potential response

In deciding whether your case meets the above criteria it is useful to consider how others might respond to the details. A review of the literature may indicate that your case is rare or unusual, but a literature review is time consuming and expensive. It may be more helpful initially to describe the patient to two or three colleagues of varying seniority and see what their responses are. Thereafter, verbal presentation at a departmental meeting will help refine your product. What is rare in one hospital, however, may be commonplace in another because of differences in referral patterns. What seems unusual may be relatively routine elsewhere, and sooner or later it will be necessary to do a literature search. It is also necessary to ensure that the motive for publishing the case is not self aggrandisement. It is the patient who should be interesting, not the author's skill in diagnosis or management.

Many modern case reports describe complications and these can produce a range of responses. Ideally, such a report should make the reader grateful that he or she was not involved but intrigued at what happened. It should indicate also how the problem can be avoided in the future. However, it is but a small step from here to the reader feeling that somebody (and sometimes everybody) involved in the management of the patient made a complete mess of it. Thus the report may extend a publication list, but do nothing for professional reputation! Conversely, in these audit conscious days we are being encouraged more to "own up" when things go wrong, and such reports have merit in them if the message is clear to others. The *British Medical Journal* encourages this under the general heading of "Lesson of the Week."

How to report

Having established that your case is of interest to others you need to ensure that the material is presented in a fashion that will make others share your interest. It is probably wise to start by writing down (for your initial verbal presentation) the details of the case, then develop the discussion, and finally add the other components. However, this is not the way in which the reader will encounter the report and the overall sequence must be kept in mind throughout.

Title

Most journal readers decide which papers they are going to read by skimming the titles. If the title of a case report is too full the reader may feel that it has said all there is to know. Ideally the title should be short, descriptive, and eye catching.

Authorship

Establishing authorship is an increasing problem in medical publication and this applies particularly to case reports. Only one person actually writes a paper and the other authors of a case report should probably be restricted to those who had a significant input to the management of those aspects that were unusual. Thus a case report written by two or three individuals may be reasonable, but it is difficult to see any justification for a list of five or six authors describing the management of one patient. This smacks of ego "massaging" in the interest of the future advancement of the first named author.

Introduction

There is a tendency to write a short history of the condition when introducing a case report, but this is either unnecessary material or should be put in the discussion. Certainly the introduction may be used to place the case in context or indicate its relevance, but there is often no reason to have an opening section at all. The report may begin simply with the case description.

Case description

In writing the core part of the paper it is essential to keep to the basic rules of clinical practice. The details will vary a little according to the specialty, but the report should be chronological and detail the presenting history, examination findings, and investigation results before going on to describe the patient's progress. The description should be complete, but the real skill is to accentuate the positive features without obscuring them in a mass of negative and mostly irrelevant findings. Consider what questions of fact a colleague might ask (this is one reason for an initial verbal presentation) and ensure that the answers are clearly within the report. Illustrations can be particularly helpful, and in some circumstances they are essential. A photograph of the patient or of the equipment used, line diagrams of operative procedures, graphs of physiological measurements, and summary tables of events can all, when used appropriately, add much to the reader's understanding.

Never forget that it is a patient who is being described, not a case, and that confidentiality must be absolute. Age, occupation, and geographical location might be all that a determined journalist requires to identify the patient, yet such information can be essential to the report. Similarly, blanking over the eyes may be sufficient to obscure identity only if the reader does not know the individual. Increasingly, it may be wise to obtain written consent from the patient at an early stage in the preparation of the report, particularly if photographic material is to be used. Some journals now insist on this.

Discussion

In preparing a report of an unusual condition it is often tempting to expand the paper and produce a review of the literature, particularly if a great deal of work has been put into gathering all the published information on the condition, but it is a temptation that should be resisted (by editors as well as authors). If a review is merited it should be written as an entirely separate exercise by a much more experienced author than is usual for a case report.

The main purpose of the discussion is to explain how and why decisions were made and what lesson is to be learnt from *this* experience. It may require some reference to other cases but, again, the tendency to produce a review must be resisted. The aim should be to refine and define the message for the reader. The good case report will make it quite clear how such a case would be tackled in the future.

References

As indicated, reference to the work of others should be made only where it is necessary to make a clear point. If a standard textbook has indicated that one line of treatment should have been followed, then it should be quoted. Reports by others should be mentioned only where they actively support (or contradict) the particular experience and conclusion.

No matter how exhaustive the search of the literature has been, it is possible that something may have been missed out. It is a very brave, and perhaps foolhardy, author who claims absolute priority in the description of some clinical phenomenon.

Acknowledgements

Acknowledging the assistance and support of others is almost as difficult an area as deciding who should be among the authors of a case report. The key question is whether the patient would have been managed, or the paper written, without the assistance of that specific individual. A particular problem is deciding whether it is necessary to thank the consultant or other individual clinically responsible for the patient for permission to publish details. With the increasing tendency to seek permission from the patient it would seem that this rather old fashioned practice can be allowed to die out.

Where to publish

A provisional decision about which journal the report will be submitted to should be made before starting to write. The next stage must be to read the guide to contributors. Journals vary in style and it is helpful to try and picture how the report will appear as it is prepared. The author should always aim for a peer reviewed journal and one which he or she already reads regularly. Familiarity with the journal will provide a better idea of what the editor and thus the readers find interesting, and this will help with the whole process of preparation.

Thereafter, the decision is going to lie between a general, specialist, and even subspecialty journal. The choice will depend on the rarity of the case and its specific features. Keep in mind the basic reason for writing a case report: namely, that it should have a message for the reader. Decide what the message is, consider who the message is aimed at, and then select a journal whose readership will include the target audience.

Guidelines for a case report

- The report should detail
  What happened to the patient
  The time course of events
  Why the particular management was chosen
- There may be no need for an opening section. Begin with the case description if possible
- Positive features should be accentuated and irrelevant details avoided
- A photograph or other illustration may be useful
- Confidentiality must be absolute
- The discussion should be useful and not overlong
- Reference other work only when necessary to make a specific point
- Cases that really merit publication always have an educational message

---

The final stages of preparation

Once the first draft is written, it should be put away for a week or two, then refined and revised several times. Reading aloud, first in private and later to one or two others who have not heard the case before, is invaluable. This will help improve the clarity of the report and its English, as well as bringing out any inconsistencies of fact or interpretation. The text should be checked and rechecked for errors in spelling, punctuation, and adherence to the journal's instructions on style. Finally, the requisite number of clear copies, correctly paginated, should be sent with a polite covering letter to the editor, and accompanied by a silent prayer that the next issue of that journal does not contain an identical case!

11 How to write a review

LEO STRUNIN

Review articles are very popular. Editors like them because they know that, along with editorials and the correspondence column, review articles are among the most widely read parts of scientific journals. Readers like reviews because they are part of the solution to the problem of keeping up with the ever expanding medical literature. However, for the writer, the review is one of the more difficult forms of communication.

Most commonly, reviews are written by invitation. This invitation may come from the editor of a "traditional journal," which may be defined as one publishing a combination of editorials, original work, a correspondence column, and reviews, or from a member of an editorial team who specifically commissions reviews. In addition, there are journals and "magazines" entirely devoted to review articles, and again, most of these obtain their material by invitation. There is, of course, nothing to prevent an author sending an unsolicited review to any journal. In general, such a review is not as likely to succeed in being published as one which has been requested. If you wish to write an unsolicited review, it is advisable to contact the editor of the journal of your choice ahead of time to ascertain whether the subject matter is appropriate. This will also allow the editor to decide, without offence, on your suitability to write the review and let you know if the topic has already been commissioned elsewhere, or whether such a review is in the publication pipeline. Many peer review journals have specific postgraduate issues where a series of articles on a given topic is commissioned.

As with all other scientific manuscripts, the best place to publish a review is in a peer reviewed journal. The "by invitation" journals which focus entirely on reviews are not always subject to manuscript peer review and this policy has been severely criticised.[1] In addition, there are review articles, usually short, which are commissioned by drug or other commercial companies specifically on their products. These are not usually peer reviewed and may be biased.

What are the characteristics of a good reviewer?

In general the reviewer will be an expert in the chosen field. Commonly, reviewers come from the academic ranks, but this is not an essential requirement. However, considerable time and access to extensive library facilities are needed to produce a good piece of work. There is also an element of psychological preparation, particularly when reviewing a complex topic. This may require the ability of a person to be away from the normal working environment and not subject to interruptions from colleagues, telephone calls, etc; this is more likely with an academic position rather than in busy clinical practice.

How will a topic for a review be chosen?

In general, subjects are suggested by the person commissioning the review, although topics may be suggested by an individual, who then approaches an editor about writing a review on their own topic. The main reason for recruiting a recognised authority on the subject under consideration is that the best reviews have both a national and international context. Clearly, considerable experience and authority are required to review in this manner. However, individuals who fit this description are often very heavily committed elsewhere and are reluctant, sometimes, to undertake a review alone. As a result, it is increasingly common for a senior author to write in conjunction with a more junior colleague. It is worth noting that there is a dynamic relationship between people who write together. Even if the junior member of the partnership does the "gophering," it must be clear that the review is a joint effort and that the expertise of the more senior author is brought to bear in order to produce a good piece of work.

Where will the review material come from?

Clearly, selecting authors who are experts in their fields means that they will have at their disposal much of the material which will form the basis of a review. In addition, they will have the contacts to obtain information not readily accessible to the novice. However, in these days of computer literature searching, it is obviously essential that a literature search be conducted to ensure that essential references are not missed. It is helpful in the review for the search methods used to be outlined. There should always be a series of primary references so that the reader can look up the basic material of the topic. Other important factors are the criteria of the reviewing of methods and source material. The criteria should be included in the review so that readers may form their own opinions as to the validity of the work.

Although computer searching of the literature with key words is extremely helpful, they commonly will not discover all of a given topic. Serendipity is an important factor. This means that the reviewer must visit the library, because often things are picked up, purely by chance during a manual search, that are related to the topic but are not revealed by the computer search. Any contentious points which are included in a review should be referenced. Unpublished observations and personal communications should be considered carefully since these cannot be verified by the reader. But if they represent important information they may be permissible. In addition, reference to work that is "in press," particularly in journals which are not commonly available in departmental libraries, should be limited. Again, if the information is new and important, an exception may be made.

How should the contents of the review be laid out?

Box 1 illustrates a logical order approach so that the reader may follow the review in the best manner. The topic of the review should be outlined right at the beginning. If appropriate, the historical background should be given. If basic science, methodology, and animal studies are appropriate they should be given next, carefully delineating the pros and cons of each item and giving the key references. Any human studies should follow, and then the discussion. The conclusions should not be based on personal opinions unless this is made very clear. Recommendations, if appropriate, are extremely helpful for the reader since they will bring the review together in summary form. Any unresolved problems should be included. Speculation about the future may encourage the reader to conduct further study.

BOX 1: The review contents: logical order

1 What is the problem?	6 Human studies
2 Historical background	7 Discussion
3 Basic science	8 Conclusions
4 Methodology	9 Recommendations
5 Animal studies	10 The future

In addition to following a logical order, the review should contain a glossary of terms. This is particularly necessary if new items are introduced or the topic has items which may be unfamiliar to the general reader. Abbreviations should be used only if they are recognised ones. Each item should be spelt out in full initially with the abbreviation following it in brackets. Unrecognised abbreviations should not be used. If there are complex mathematical considerations, methodology, or details of experimental designs etc, these may be placed more appropriately in appendices at the end of the review article, and merely noted in the text, so as not to interrupt the flow for the reader.

Many journals will ask for an abstract or summary to go with the review. As this may be the first or only part of the review that will be read it must be accurate. Rather disturbingly, when 83 reports were studied using six criteria to determine similarities and differences in abstracts and summaries, the authors came to the conclusion that important items had been omitted in the abstract or summary, or both, in 20% of cases.[2] Although abstracts were 30% longer than summaries, they were repetitious, and there was sufficient overlap that either the abstract or the summary was superfluous. It is also of interest that these authors published a subsequent erratum[3] on their own paper.[2]

How should you produce the manuscript?

It is very important that you follow the journal's instructions to authors. In particular, the number of words should be adhered to, and if it is likely that you are going to exceed the recommended number this must be discussed with the editor ahead of time; generally the average A4 or letter standard paper, double spaced, will have approximately 300 words per page. The instructions to authors will give clear information as to how references should be laid out and how many there should be. It is not necessary to reference every single part of the review; nevertheless any contentious issues should be referenced, as well as the key publications and items which have been used to form the basis of the review. Tables and figures should conform to the instructions to authors, and the number of these should be limited to that requested. If tables or figures are to be reproduced from any copyright material then permission in writing must be obtained from the copyright holder. This is usually the publisher of the material rather than the authors.

The manuscript should be produced with a good quality printer. This means having access to either a laser or ink jet printer or a near letter quality dot matrix printer. Dot matrix printers without near letter quality do not produce text which is easy to read or photocopy. Most text these days is produced with word processing programs, and most of these have a spell checker. This should be used frequently during preparation of the manuscript to make certain that there are no errors in the text, though watch out for misspellings that are accepted by the checker as words.

The typeface used should be a serif typeface (for example, Times Roman), rather than a sanserif (for example, Helvetica), because sanserif is more difficult to read when used for text. Sanserif typeface is suitable for figures and tables. The point size should be at least 12 point (72 points=1 inch), as this makes the text easier to read. Some journals are willing to accept manuscripts on computer disk or by modem, but most journals still also request a printed version. The arrangement for transferring manuscripts should be ascertained with the journal ahead of time. You should always check how many copies of the manuscript are required by the journal, and you should keep a copy of what is actually sent to the journal to check for changes in the future.

One critical aspect of a review is the references. These should be accurate and carefully checked with regard to authors' names, the title, volume number, year, and page numbers. The style and format of the requesting journal must be adhered to. Most scientific journals use the Vancouver style, which means that the references are numbered in the text and then laid out, either in numerical or alphabetical order, at the end of the text. The Vancouver style includes the names of all authors, although some journals may limit this; the title of the journal; the full title of the article, the year of publication, volume number, and first and last page numbers. In addition, when a book, monograph, or chapter is referenced, then the names of both the authors and the editor(s), as well as the publisher's name and town of origin, are needed to complete the references.

It cannot be emphasised too strongly that the references must be checked extremely carefully. There is nothing more frustrating for the reader than, having read your review and come across an interesting reference, to then go to the library and find that the citation is untraceable.

Can we describe the ideal review? Box 2 indicates some "do's and don'ts" which may be helpful.

BOX 2: The ideal review

Should be:	Should not be:
Topical	Old hat
Up to date	A twelfth review out of eleven
Balanced	others
Accurate	A personal view only
Authoritative	Anecdotal
Quotable	Superficial
Provocative	Out of context
A good read	Boring

Accuracy in quoting other people's work is vital. That errors can occur is well documented. For example, in a study of 96 references from one year of review articles, randomly selected to see if they agreed with review article statements, 39 of 165 statements in the articles (24%) were wrong or inappropriate.[4]

Deadlines for reviews tend to be flexible and this may encourage laziness. The balance between getting it right and inordinate delay, and maybe lack of topicality or being beaten at the post by someone else, can be difficult to achieve. There is often an initial impetus and enthusiasm for a subject which once lost is difficult to resurrect. One benefit of writing with a co-author is that the pressure to finish may be maintained.

Once the manuscript is completed to the author's satisfaction there is some advantage in showing it to a colleague, perhaps in an unrelated field, for comment. The requisite number of copies should then be sent to the requesting editor. Depending on the journal, the peer review process may vary. Some may treat your manuscript as any other submitted paper and you will receive in due course the reviewer's and editor's comments. Alternatively the peer review process may only be between the editor and yourself.

Is there any difference between a review and a chapter?

A book chapter is more of a personal statement and may be much more wide ranging in its topic than a review, which tends to be more focused. Original data are not normally included in either chapters or review articles, where others' data are referenced and referred to, rather than new information being included. You can ask more provocative questions in a review, since you may be attempting to encourage others to do research in areas which are not completed. A chapter in a textbook is usually more a statement of the current state of development in a particular area rather than the latest cutting edge.

In summary, a good review should, on any particular topic, help the reader to discern the relevant pros and cons easily and have the key references for confirmation and further information. The reader should also feel that your opinion is of value in deciding which, if any, of the conflicting views are most acceptable on the balance of available information; and where there is no clear consensus further research may be suggested.

---

[1] Søreide E, Steen PA. Danger of review articles. *BMJ* 1993; **306**: 66–7.
[2] Didolkar MS, Fleming MV, Venazi WE Jr. Abstract renders the summary superfluous. *Surg Gynecol Obstet* 1989; **168**: 259–62.
[3] Didolkar MS, Fleming MV, Venazi WE Jr. Erratum. *Surg Gynecol Obstet* 1989; **169**: 178.
[4] Neihouse PF, Priske SC. Quotation accuracy in review articles. *Drug Intelligence in Clinical Practice* 1989; **23**: 594–6.

12 The role of the editor

G SMITH

Objectives of the journal

The function of the journal is determined by the editorial board of the journal. The editorial board extends to the editor broad guidelines on the type of journal which the editor should produce. For example, the purpose of the *British Journal of Anaesthesia* is the publication of original work in all branches of anaesthesia, including the application of basic sciences. In addition, the journal publishes review articles and reports of new equipment.

The journal may be a weekly or monthly publication of a specialised or general nature. These features may have an important impact on editorial policy—for example, the necessity for specialist assessors' opinions.

Editorial policy

The editor should have formulated a policy for implementing the objectives of the journal.

Policy for authors

The editor should ensure that all correspondence with authors is dealt with rapidly, effectively, and courteously. Assessors' reports should be obtained expeditiously and transmitted rapidly to the authors. In particular, assessors' reports should be detailed, meticulous, and of high quality. If the manuscript is rejected as being unsuitable for publication, the assessors' comments should be seen by the authors to be fair and acceptable.

Policy for readers

The editor attempts to incorporate in each issue of the journal at least some article, be it editorial, original article, book review, or correspondence, that will appeal to any reader of the journal. Articles should be up to date and of high scientific quality, represent the leading edge of scientific progress, and be composed in good quality English which is as comprehensible as possible to the general reader.[1]

Balance of the journal's contents

Material published in a monthly scientific journal may be classified under the various sections described in box 1. As part of his or her general policy, the editor must determine the balance of contents in each section of each issue of the journal. This is determined to a large extent by the nature of the material submitted to the journal but, none the less, the editor does exercise considerable influence on the overall contents of the journal.

BOX 1: Classification of contents of monthly scientific journals
- Editorial(s)
- Original articles:
    Clinical investigations
    Laboratory investigations
- Short (rapid) communications
- Review article(s)
- Case report(s)
- Commentary
- Historical articles
- Apparatus
- Book reviews
- Correspondence
- Proceedings (or abstracts) or meetings of scientific societies

---

Editorials

These may be commissioned as reviews or critiques of original articles accepted for publication in the journal. Alternatively, an editorial may be thought appropriate to describe briefly a subject which does not warrant a full review, or to draw attention to very recent innovations. Editorials are particularly appropriate for complementing original articles which either do not present a balanced view of current opinion or require interpretation for the benefit of the general reader.

The editor may publish any number of editorials in each issue of the journal. This distinguishes the way in which different editors imprint their own personality on a scientific journal.

Original articles

These are the mainstay of the monthly scientific journal. The editor may change the character of the journal by policies favouring particular areas of research (for example, changing the balance between clinical and non-clinical research, or between basic and applied science) or by encouraging submission of articles in a specific area (for example, intensive care) at the expense of more general articles.

Review articles

These may be either commissioned or uninvited submissions. Again, editors have considerable latitude in pursuing their own policies in respect of the quantity and direction of review material, within the constraints laid down by the editorial board. Editors may decide to subject submitted review material to peer review or take their own decisions on the quality of such articles.

Case reports

These often present considerable difficulties to the editor. In a monthly scientific journal with a low acceptance rate for submitted articles, particularly stringent criteria may apply. For acceptance in the *British Journal of Anaesthesia*, case reports must present a unique problem or reiterate a problem of outstanding importance—for example, relating to anaesthetic mortality.

Other categories

In addition to the above categories, other material may be accepted under a variety of headings—apparatus, laboratory investigations, equipment, history, commentary, etc. Again, the decision to accept such materials and the balance of acceptance reflects editorial personality.

Book reviews

There is little doubt that book reviews are informative and often sought out more avidly by readers than other sections of the journal.

Invariably, such reviews are obtained only by invitation; unsolicited reviews are always rejected.

Correspondence

The correspondence section of the journal is extremely important and the editor will attempt to encourage lively and informative debate. Usually, most correspondence relates to published articles in the journal. This section may also be used for floating new hypotheses and particularly for drawing attention to important hazards, because the submission to publication interval is shorter for this section than any other in the journal. The correspondence section should not be used for abbreviated case reports or shortened original investigations which attempt to avoid peer review.

Organisation of the editorial team

Manuscripts submitted to a monthly peer reviewed scientific journal are normally processed by a team rather than a single individual. The editor (occasionally termed the editor in chief) determines the way in which his or her team functions.

Essentially there are two major methods of organising the editorial team (fig 1).

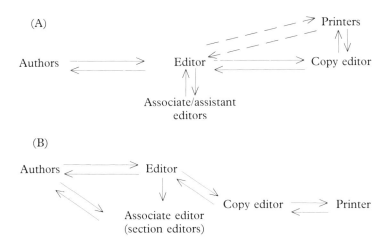

Figure 1 Organisation of the editorial team. In the first mode (A) the editor is the sole conduit of communication with authors and copy editors. In the second mode (B) associate editors (or section editors) may be given full responsibility for processing manuscripts.

In system (A) the editor acts as the sole final conduit between acceptance of manuscripts in the editorial office and onward transmission to the copy editor or publishers.

In system (B) several individuals may act as conduits between submission of manuscripts and transmission to the publishers. In this system, manuscripts relating to particular subspecialities may be handled semi-independently by section editors—for example, in anaesthesia there may be section editors for manuscripts covering the specialities of intensive care, obstetric anaesthesia, pain, cardiac anaesthesia, etc.

These two types of editorial organisation have specific advantages and disadvantages. In the first system, there is greater uniformity of criteria for accepting and rejecting manuscripts and greater uniformity in subediting; the disadvantage is a much higher workload for the individual editor. In the second system, the workload is spread between several individuals, and such editors may exhibit greater insight within their own specialised fields; however, the disadvantage is greater lack of uniformity of acceptance criteria and editing.

Processing of manuscripts

Initial screening

Before seeking expert assessors' views on the manuscript, the editor should ensure that some basic formalities have been completed.

(1) The manuscript should conform to the uniform requirements for manuscripts submitted to biomedical journals.[2] In this agreement, it is stated that a manuscript must be accompanied by a covering letter signed by all authors of the manuscript. The letter should include information on prior or duplicate publication, or submission elsewhere, of any part of the work.

(2) There should be a statement of financial or other relationships that might lead to conflict of interests.

(3) There should be a statement that the manuscript has been read and approved by all authors.

(4) The name, address, and telephone number of the corresponding author should be noted.

(5) Each manuscript should be presented in the standard format (box 2).

BOX 2: Typical layout of a scientific manuscript

- Title page
- Summary, including key words
- Introduction
- Methods
- Results
- Discussion
- Acknowledgements
- List of references
- Tables (including legends to tables)
- Legends to illustration

Pages should be numbered in the top right hand corner, the title page being 1, etc.

The editor also initially ensures that the contents of the manuscript are appropriate for his or her particular journal; for example, if the journal is a predominantly clinical one, manuscripts relating to basic laboratory investigations may automatically be returned to the authors without formal assessment.

Assessors' reports

After the initial screening, the editor seeks expert advice on the quality of the paper. Advice may be sought from one, two, three, or occasionally more expert assessors. The assessor is asked particularly if the work is original and if the experimental methodology is sufficiently accurate and reproducible to generate data on which sound conclusions may be based. Advice may be offered to the assessors in the form of standard guidelines (box 3). Assessors may be asked to produce an anonymous report for transmission to the author and also to complete advisory guidelines confidential to the editor.

Review of assessors' reports

Armed with the benefit of assessors' advice and his or her own review of the manuscript, the editor may draw three conclusions:
(1) The manuscript is unacceptable for publication and is unlikely to be modified in such a way as to become acceptable for publication. Often the major reasons for this decision are that the work is not original or that the methods of investigation are inappropriate or inaccurate. It may also become clear at this stage that the material is not appropriate for the particular journal.

(2) The manuscript is acceptable for publication either as it stands or with some minor modifications.

(3) The present manuscript is not acceptable for publication but that it *might* become acceptable for publication subject to modifications. To guide the authors as to the extent of modifications required, the editor may send the authors the assessors' confidential reports together with a covering letter (which may incorporate comments made by the assessors on the confidential report). In addition, guidance may be provided on the statistical handling of the data and editorial changes which may be required to produce conformity with the style of the journal.

The revised manuscript

The editor may decide on his or her own initiative that the manuscript is acceptable for publication or (with the benefit of clarification of questions of originality or methodology) that the

---

BOX 3: Guidelines for reviewers*

(1) The unpublished manuscript is a privileged document. Please protect it from any form of exploitation. Reviewers are expected not to cite a manuscript or refer to the work it describes before it has been published, and to refrain from using the information it contains for the advancement of their own research.

(2) A reviewer should consciously adopt a positive, impartial attitude towards the manuscript under review. Your position should be that of the author's ally, with the aim of promoting effective and accurate scientific communication.

(3) If you believe that you cannot judge a given article impartially, please return the manuscript immediately to the editor with that explanation.

(4) Reviews should be completed expeditiously, within 2–3 weeks. If you know that you cannot finish the review within the time specified, please inform the editor to determine what action should be taken.

(5) A reviewer should not discuss a paper with its author.

(6) Please do not make any specific statement about the acceptability of a paper in your comments for transmission to the author, but advise the editor on the sheet provided.

(7) In your review, please consider the following aspects of the manuscript as far as they are applicable:
Importance of the question or subject studied
Originality of the work

---

paper is quite clearly unacceptable for publication. If additional expert advice is required the editor may seek further reports from the original or new assessors.

Editorial decision

It is important to emphasise that the assessors' reports represent only guidelines for the editor and they do not dictate the editor's course of action. Editorial decisions are based upon editorial policy, assessors' reports, the assessors' confidential comments to the editor, the editor's reading of the manuscript, the flow of manuscripts to the journal, and constraints imposed by the size of the journal. As only a relatively small proportion of manuscripts may be instantaneously deemed acceptable or unacceptable for publication, the editor may rely heavily upon his or her judgment of what represents an advance on our current state of knowledge and the degree to which confirmation is required. For example, when a new drug is

---

Appropriateness of approach or experimental design
Adequacy of experimental techniques (including statistics where appropriate)
Soundness of conclusions and interpretation
Relevance of discussion
Clarity of writing and soundness of organisation of the paper

(8) In comments intended for the author's eyes, criticism should be presented dispassionately, and abrasive remarks avoided.

(9) Suggested revisions should be couched as such, and not expressed as conditions of acceptance. On the sheet provided, please distinguish between revisions considered essential and those judged merely desirable.

(10) Your criticisms, arguments, and suggestions concerning the paper will be most useful to the editor if they are carefully documented.

(11) You are not requested to correct deficiencies of style or mistakes in grammar, but any help you can offer to the editor in this regard will be appreciated.

(12) A reviewer's recommendations are gratefully received by the editor, but since editorial decisions are usually based on evaluations derived from several sources, a reviewer should not expect the editor to honour his or her every recommendation.

* These guidelines were prepared by the Council of Biology Editors.

introduced for the treatment of a particular disease it is important that several centres, probably in different countries, provide confirmatory evidence of the pharmacological and therapeutic action of that drug. However, there comes a time when additional studies are not required, and then they may be rejected on the grounds that they do not represent an advance in our current state of knowledge.

Editing the manuscript

After accepting a manuscript for publication, the editor may either edit the manuscript himself or herself or pass it to an associate editor for this purpose. The process of editing follows certain principles.

(1) An attempt is made to shorten the manuscript without any loss of accuracy. Authors often repeat data in the results and discussion section of a manuscript. Repetition is common in a concluding paragraph or indeed if a summary is appended to the manuscript. In my experience, the commonest form of repetition is where the same data appear in both tables and figures (often because the tables have been used as part of a verbal presentation to a learned society).

(2) Where manuscripts have emanated from non-English speaking countries, considerable effort may be required to correct English grammar.

(3) The editor may change phrases or sentences to standardise to a particular "house style"—for example, use of the term "tracheal tube" rather than "endotracheal tube."

(4) The references may be checked for accuracy and validity.

(5) The manuscript is standardised in respect of drug names, symbols, units, and abbreviations. Frequently, this work is undertaken by a professional subeditor (or copy editor).

Copy editing

Having finished with the manuscript, the editor passes it on to a copy editor who marks up the manuscript to guide the printer on how to typeset the manuscript. The copy editor may also undertake a large amount of editing.

Proof stage

Proofs from the printer are sent to the copy editor, the authors, and the editors, all of whom make corrections. These are passed on to the copy editor, who collates the corrections and transmits a corrected proof to the printer.

Page proofs

Final page proofs are seen usually only by the editor and copy editor.

Publication

It will be clear from the foregoing that the process of publishing a scientific manuscript is complex and time consuming (fig 2). For a monthly journal, therefore, it should be anticipated that many months will elapse between submission of a manuscript and its eventual publication.

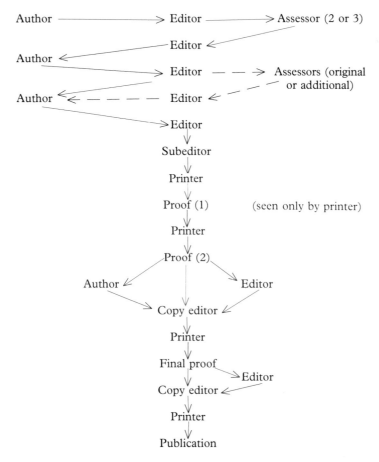

Figure 2 Stages in the progress of a manuscript from submission to publication.

Other published material

As the editor is responsible for assessing every word which appears in the journal, it is necessary for him or her to review all material, including advertisements, for both commercial or academic purposes. Commercial advertisements must be closely vetted to ensure that outrageous claims or inaccuracies are avoided, and academic advertisements assessed for accuracy in so far as it is possible.

[1] Extended guide to contributors. *British Journal of Anaesthesia* 1990; **64**: 129–36.
[2] International Committee of Medical Journal Editors. Uniform requirements for manuscripts submitted to biomedical journals. *BMJ* 1988; **296**: 401–5.

13 The role of the manuscript assessor

MICHAEL J CURTIS, MICHAEL J SHATTOCK

The role of the manuscript assessor in the peer review system is twofold. On behalf of the journal, the assessor advises the editor on whether a manuscript is suitable for publication. As well, the assessor provides feedback to the authors. Manuscript assessment can be viewed from two perspectives: what the journal intends the assessor to do, and what the assessor understands his or her job to be. The objective of this chapter is to summarise the essential features of a good review that provides both a readily digestible assessment of the manuscript for the editor and a fair and constructive critique for the authors. We have examined the assessor's role from these two perspectives.

The role of an assessor

The assessor ideally writes his or her report according to the instruction given by the journal. Many journals have very specific rules regarding what should be dealt with in their comments to the author and what should be said only in confidence to the editor. Thus, the assessor usually has two forms to fill in—one for the author and one for the editor. A responsible assessor will be aware that the editor is primarily interested in the "bottom line"—that is, whether the manuscript should be accepted, returned to the author for revision, or rejected. Many editors will ask the assessor to advise formally on the bottom line by ticking boxes to rank the manuscript according to specific criteria (which vary from journal to journal). Generally the assessor will make this assessment, which is highly subjective, on his or her "gut feeling" after reading the manuscript.

From the initial glance at the manuscript, and throughout the careful section by section assessment, the assessor will keep a mental tally of "points for" and "points against." The importance of these subjective rankings of a manuscript can be assessed from chapter 12. Most assessors will be aware that the confidential comments to the editors will determine the fate of the manuscript, which ultimately will be acceptance or rejection. Since the editor will base the decision on these confidential comments, it is essential that the assessor does not send contradictory signals to the authors in the specific critique.

Few manuscripts are accepted without revision (see below for specific criteria for determining the assessor's decision) so the assessor essentially has to decide whether to induce the editor to encourage the author to resubmit a revised manuscript or to try another journal. The revised manuscript can be expected to be accepted, provided the author chooses to respond positively to the assessor's comments. Therefore, the assessor should have the ultimate accept/reject decision in mind, even if manuscript revision is requested. The interesting part of manuscript assessment, then, relates to the attitudes of an individual assessor which determine the criteria he or she, as an individual, uses to make his accept/reject decision. This will be discussed again later. However, we will first run through the idealised process of manuscript assessment by considering the individual sections of a typical manuscript.

The abstract

After considering the overall presentation of the manuscript, the abstract is the first section that influences the assessor; if it is well written he or she proceeds with a positive attitude. The points the assessor looks for are listed in the box.

BOX 1: Important points that are assessed in the abstract
- A clear and stated hypothesis or objective
- Methods appropriate for achievement of the objectives
- Understandable and believable results
- Results which reveal all that is necessary for the study objectives to be achieved
- Conclusions which are a fair reflection of the data
- An overall impression that the study seems interesting, worthwhile, and important

If there appear to be problems in one or more of these areas of the abstract, the assessor will be set against the manuscript to a greater or lesser degree, from the start. This setback for the author can be rectified only if it transpires that the rest of the manuscript is reasonable and the shortcomings of the manuscript are restricted to the abstract (that is, are a question of presentation). If, in addition, the English is poor or there are typographical errors in the abstract then the assessor will immediately tend to take a dim view of the manuscript and may be daunted by the prospect of ploughing through the remainder of it.

The introduction

The initial impressions gained by the assessor from the abstract will be reinforced or negated by the contents of the introduction. Here, additional factors not evaluable from the abstract will come into play. The most important of these is the question of interest; the assessor will expect the stage to be set for the study in the introduction. The most important component of this is the question: what is it that the authors are interested in finding out? Thus the assessor is looking for a clear statement of a gap in scientific knowledge which requires further study. If the authors fail to "sell" their study by identifying a worthwhile question then the manuscript is likely to be rejected. Also, the introduction should contain a synopsis of the approach to be taken. If this synopsis fails to identify a reasonable approach to the question then the manuscript is likely to be rejected.

The methods

If there are no problems of the nature discussed above then the assessor will examine the methods section for a clear exposition of how the question set out earlier was approached. In animal studies the species, housing conditions, age, and weight of the animals should be given. An indication of how animals were assigned to groups (that is, method of randomisation) is necessary (although this is commonly overlooked by both author and assessor). The group sizes should be given. This is often a good indication of the scientific validity of study design because unequal group sizes often mean that randomisation was not part of the study design. Where possible, exclusion criteria should be defined and the reviewer should be able to see that application of these criteria does not introduce an element of bias in the data collection. The techniques used should be up to date. Clearly, any technique which is outmoded (or, worse, previously shown to be inappropriate) may lead to the manuscript being rejected. The means of statistical analysis should be appropriate; although this aspect has been notoriously weak in the past in the biological literature, assessors are becoming much more skilled in evaluating whether numerical analysis has been performed appropriately. A guide to methods and analysis (with special reference to studies of cardiac arrhythmias) has been published.

The results

The assessor will be particularly interested in how the data are presented. Legible, rational figures are essential. It is surprising how bizarre some figures may be in initial submissions of manuscripts. Excessive use of abbreviations (abs) and acronyms (i.r.r.i.t.a.t.i.n.g.) can render a manuscript unintelligible (and often unreadable). A common error is to present data in figures or tables, then to repeat the same numerical data in the text. The assessor's immediate response to this is to suspect that the manuscript is short of data. The text presenting the results is often a source of immense annoyance to the assessor, especially if it constitutes little more than a running legend to the figures and tables. If the assessor does not feel that this text leads the reader by the hand through the data, this can often lead to a rejection.

Finally, statements which mislead are unacceptable. One typical example of this is the statement that drug X reduced variable Y but that the change "failed to achieve a level of statistical significance"; this sort of statement shows that the author is prepared to believe in drug effects in the face of statistical evidence that none exist. A loss of faith by the assessor in the author's objectivity will inevitably follow, and the manuscript may be rejected.

The discussion

The assessor has by now made a judgment of the manuscript. His or her initial gut feeling will have been reinforced, or possibly changed. The assessor will, in particular, have to come to conclusions about the data, and so will be looking for a concise and well referenced reiteration of this understanding. If, instead, the discussion presents hypotheses and lines of argument to explain or interpret the data which are unexpected (with reference to the introduction and the results themselves) then the assessor is likely to respond negatively. Vague and unsubstantiated statements count against the author. A logical and succinct argument is required. Also, the assessor will expect all the data in the results section to be discussed, especially the anomalous data; failure to acknowledge and address anomalies will ensure that the manuscript is rejected. Style, too, is important. Let us make this quite clear: bombastic, opinionated, and bumptious prose will not be tolerated under any circumstances since, as with this sentence, the tone is not appropriate. Misrepresentation of the literature to suit the author's prejudices will also meet with opposition from the assessor.

BOX 2: Important points that are assessed

The introduction:
- Must identify the gap in knowledge that warranted the study
- Should give a synopsis of the approach taken to the question, which must be reasonable

The methods:
- Should clearly describe how the question was approached
- Group sizes should be given and exclusion criteria defined if possible
- Techniques used should be up to date
- Statistical analyses should be appropriate

The results:
- Should use appropriate, legible figures
- Figures and tables should not repeat data in the text

The discussion:
- Should not give unexpected hypotheses
- Should not be vague or give unsubstantiated statements
- Should discuss the data and address anomalies

What actually happens

In most cases the scenario described above is what actually happens. However, this is not always so. The first, and most immediate, deviation from ideal assessor behaviour is that the assessor may be overly influenced by the presentation and appearance of a manuscript. Even the most excellent study will be disadvantaged if it is untidily presented. In an ideal world, assessors would maintain their objectivity irrespective of the presentation and layout of the manuscript (after all, it is the science they are supposed to be assessing, not the quality of the laser printer). However, not unreasonably, many assessors subconsciously associate an untidy manuscript with a sloppy approach to science. The onus, therefore, is clearly on authors to prepare their manuscripts in such a way that assessors find them pleasant to read. Having to struggle through pages of single spaced text that refers to complex and poorly designed figures or large, unwieldy tables is guaranteed to place any assessor in a less than favourable frame of mind. On the other hand, although a poorly presented manuscript may indeed reflect lack of attention to detail, the assessor should avoid the temptation to assume that a well presented manuscript automatically reflects a well constructed study.

Another problem is that the assessor often lapses into inconsistencies. Some assessors, in their confidential comments to the editor, have been known to recommend rejection on the grounds that, for example, "this is a boring study, with inappropriate methods, unbelievable results, and incomprehensible discussion" while starting their comments to the authors with, "This is an interesting study that is worthy of publication." When the manuscript is rejected the authors then respond with an indignant letter saying, "but the reviewer said it was interesting and should be published." The motivation behind such behaviour is obscure, yet, as editors ourselves, we have seen it (the above is a verbatim example). Most journals specifically request assessors not to indicate their recommendation of acceptance or rejection. This, however, does not absolve the assessor from providing justification to the authors for any negative confidential recommendation to the editor. In reviewing a manuscript, the assessor should therefore try to provide substantive justification in the comments to authors for any condemnation in the comments to editors.

Unfortunately, scientists are human beings and occasional misconduct does occur. Assessors tend to be experts in the subject of the submitted manuscript and may therefore have a vested interest in seeing the manuscript accepted for publication (if it suppports the assessor's viewpoint and, especially, if it cites fulsomely the assessor's own work) or rejected (if it undermines the assessor's previous or ongoing work). Occasionally it has been brought to our attention that serious misconduct has been suspected, whereby a manuscript is kept by an assessor for many months then rejected, only for a similar piece of work to be published by the assessor. Of course it is not possible to prove such things, since the author does not know the identity of the assessor and can only surmise it on the basis of events. Many assessors conscientiously devote much time and care to reviewing manuscripts, although some do not. The whole process, however, is under the ultimate control of the journal editor, and it is his or her duty to ensure that good assessors are encouraged and bad ones are weeded out of the system (see chapter 12).

Although the ultimate responsibility falls on the editor's shoulders, assessors should clearly be prepared to stand by their recommendations and criticisms. Much debate has centred on the issue of the anonymity of assessors and, although this issue is outside the scope of this chapter, it is clear that assessors must be prepared to be held accountable for their opinions. In the current peer review system, authors are also assessors and assessors are authors, so perhaps the maxim of the assessors should be, "Do unto others as you would have them do unto you." We end this chapter by concluding that, on the whole, the assessor understands the mandate and fulfils it. However, there is a case for more open (that is, non-anonymous) assessment, since this would prevent the most serious forms of misconduct.

14 What a publisher does

ALEX WILLIAMSON

Congratulations! Your paper has been accepted for publication.

At this point, the author may have his or her first contact with the publisher. In most cases this will be a fruitful collaboration, but many authors have only a vague notion of what a publisher actually does. This is evident because of the number of times I am asked, "What exactly is it that you do?"

Authors write, and the publishers provide the means for those authors to reach their audiences. The services a journal publishing house offers fall into a number of broad categories, some of which an author will have no direct contact with, but nevertheless cannot do without. The categories are: editorial, production, fulfilment, distribution, sales and marketing, and finance. Each category is dependent on the other and all work closely together.

Editorial

Within the editorial department there are two main functions—managing and commissioning and copy editing.

Mangaging and commissioning editors

Managing and commissioning editors (also called publishing managers, acquisitions editors, or sponsoring editors) are the publishers' representatives to journal editors, learned societies, and authors. The main function of a managing editor is the care of the existing list of journals. This consists of financial management, liaison with the learned society (if one is involved), overseeing the duties of the copy editor, production, advertisement sales, marketing, subscription fulfilment and distribution, and, last but by no means least, liaison and support of the journal editors. These editors are a rare breed of dedicated professionals who are often full time clinicians or academics or both. For little or no reward they devote many hours to editorial work and need strong support from the publisher.

Managing editors will also receive new journal proposals, seek specialist opinion via both questionnaires and personal contacts, analyse, research the market, cost the proposal, and, finally, present it to their management. The rejection rate for new journal proposals is very high indeed—roughly speaking, only one in ten proposals will be successful. A new journal launch requires a large investment from the publisher and so a decision to launch is never taken lightly.

The managing editor will meet the editor regularly and offer advice on publishing practice and will help in the training of support staff for the editorial office. The editor should be given a realistic budget to cover the costs of running the office in terms of postage, telephone and fax, stationery, photocopying, and secretarial assistance. Most editorial offices now run a computerised manuscript tracking system which streamlines much of the peer review procedures.

Once a manuscript is accepted for publication, the editor will send it as hard copy or on floppy disk to the publisher where it will receive the attention of the copy editor.

Copy editors

Copy editors (also called technical editors, subeditors, or production editors) provide the main link between an author and the publisher. The copy editor will prepare the accepted manuscript for press. This will not only involve mark up for the typesetter but also scrutiny of the manuscript, tables, and illustrations.

Copy editors will adapt the manuscript to the "house style" of the journal. They are concerned with details of style and ensure that spelling, grammar, punctuation, capitalisation, and mathematical conventions follow approved practice. They also look for accuracy and consistency. They pick up loose ends, discrepancies, omissions, and contradictions. Substantive queries may be referred back to the author and editor at this stage. More often the problems identified are minor and will appear as queries on the proof to the author. Copy editors will arrange relettering and redrawing of illustrations where necessary and will size them and place them appropriately in the text.

Copy editors will liaise with the typesetter and ensure that proofs are distributed quickly to authors and editors. They will proofread and collate any corrections received from authors and editors. Only in exceptional circumstances are authors allowed to make major changes to their papers at this stage, and the copy editor will refer substantive author corrections for the editor's approval.

Copy editors work to tight schedules and will often need to remind authors to return proofs promptly.

In collaboration with the editor and the advertisement department, copy editors make up the contents of each issue and pass final proofs for press. At this stage the publishing process passes to the production department.

Copyright and reprints

Either at acceptance of the manuscript for publication or at the proof stage the author will be required to assign copyright to the journal. Publishers are much better able to defend copyright than individual authors and will act on their behalf.

At proof stage authors will also be given the opportunity to purchase additional offprints of their paper (many journals will offer the author free offprints).

Production

The production staff will choose appropriate printers and typesetters for the journal, bearing in mind the budget, print run, schedule, and the use of colour illustrations and advertisements. They choose and purchase text paper and cover boards. The production department is responsible for schedules, obtains estimates, and controls costs. It keeps abreast of the latest advances in print and binding technology and will advise editorial colleagues on appropriate new means of production which will benefit the journal in terms of schedule, cost, and appearance. Overall, the production team is responsible for the look of the journal, its cost effective production on schedule, and delivery for onward distribution to the subscriber.

Fulfilment and distribution

The average specialist journal's circulation is subscription based, usually on an annual basis. By and large subscribers fall into four main categories.

(1) Institutional or library subscriptions at the full price subscription rate. Most of these sales are handled via subscription agents, who make the librarians' jobs much simpler. Librarians will probably deal with only one agent for the thousands of subscriptions they purchase. The agent will consolidate these orders and deal with the individual publishers—quite often using computers to facilitate the transfer of orders. For this service agents are given a discount by the publishers.

(2) Personal subscriptions at a discounted subscription rate.

(3) Member subscriptions. Often a journal will be owned by or published in association with a learned society. The annual membership subscription will include an automatic subscription to the society's journal.

(4) Free and exchange subscriptions. The editor and editorial board will normally receive free copies. Copyright legislation decrees that subscriptions must be deposited in the British Library and several major libraries. Subscriptions are given to the large abstracting and indexing services such as *Index Medicus, Current Contents,* and *Excerpta Medica.*

All these groups expect to receive the journal regularly, and on time, and subscribers need to be reminded each year to renew their subscriptions. Most subscription fulfilment systems are computer based and will generate mailing labels sorted into postal categories to a defined schedule. In many cases, these mailing labels will be despatched directly to the printer, who will arrange onward posting to subscribers. In other cases, publishers will handle all distribution from their own warehouses. Overseas consignments are often sent in bulk by air to a mailing house, which then organises onward distribution by that country's mail service.

The warehouse will store additional copies of the journal in order to fulfil claims for missing issues, back orders, and single copy sales.

Sales and marketing

The main source of revenue for a journal comes from the sale of paid subscriptions. However, there are other sources and I shall deal with these first before returning to the subscription area.

Advertising sales

The higher circulation general and specialist clinical journals enjoy a good revenue from the sale of display advertising space in each issue. The major space buyers are the pharmaceutical companies but equipment manufacturers and publishers also use journals to advertise their products.

The advertisement sales team not only maintains close links with agencies and companies but also liaises with the editorial team. A strong editorial policy on the percentage of advertisement versus editorial pages is needed along with a strict code on the permitted content of advertisements and their location in comparison with editorial pages.

Despite these safeguards, editors and publishers are often criticised regarding the content and placement of advertisements. Nevertheless, advertisements can provide a useful service to the reader and certainly support the journal financially.

Reprint sales

Reprint sales can be a considerable source of revenue, particularly where papers are reporting the results of clinical trials or new indications for an existing drug. Reprints should not be confused with offprints. Offprints are printed simultaneously with the journal and are primarily given free or sold at cost to authors. Reprints are produced later, usually in bulk, and are of necessity more expensive and appeal to the commercial sector.

Rights

The marketing of a journal involves not only the sale of subscriptions but also the sale of subsidiary rights. These may take the form of translation rights, rights to produce an English language edition in a slightly modified form for a foreign market, or rights to produce cheap reprints in countries where purchasing power is low.

Bulk and single copy sales

Occasionally a journal will publish a special issue or supplement on a particular "hot" topic and this may attract bulk sales from a commercial organisation or single copy sales to individuals.

Subscription sales and marketing

When a new journal is launched, the circulation climbs steadily and then plateaus as the journal is established in its specialty. Some people are of the opinion that once a journal has reached its plateau it is no longer necessary to continue active promotion. Not so! Every year an established journal will lose some 10% of its circulation owing to consolidation of library collections, budgetary restrictions, or simply a change in the direction of research in the institution. To maintain its circulation, a journal needs to be promoted to pick up new subscribers to replace those that have been lost.

In collaboration with the subscription and fulfilment department, the lapsed subscribers will be actively encouraged to renew their subscriptions and ultimately will receive a questionnaire which can provide valuable information to editorial colleagues.

The marketing department is concerned with promotion material, publicity, and advertising. It devises campaigns to promote each journal and designs, writes, and produces leaflets and catalogues which are sent by direct mail to specialists and librarians worldwide. Apart from direct mail, journals are promoted via advertisements in other relevant high circulation journals and displays at appropriate speciality meetings and symposiums.

Finance

The staff of the finance department have a number of roles—all of them concerned with money! They raise invoices, control cash flow, maintain records, and pay suppliers. The management accountant will provide monthly accounts to the senior management and will play an integral part in the constitution of annual budgets and longer term strategic planning.

Conclusion

The role of the publisher has been compared with a variety of functions—few of them favourable. We have been told we are parasites, middlemen, gamblers—to name but a few. Perhaps we are best regarded as catalysts who facilitate the communication between the authors and their readers.

15 Style—what is it, and does it matter?

NORMA PEARCE

What is style?

"Style" has a number of meanings, at least two of which are relevant to the writing and publishing of scientific papers.

Firstly, it refers to a manner of expression in language. "Have something to say and say it as clearly as you can. That is the essence of style," urged Matthew Arnold, while Jonathan Swift firmly believed that "proper words in proper places make the true definition of style."

Style may also be defined in more specific terms as the custom followed in spelling, capitalisation, punctuation, and printing arrangement and display—the house style.

The foreword to the *JAMA Stylebook* states that "a scientific journal should have a consistency of style and an accuracy of reporting on which readers come to rely. The few rules a journal adopts should be simple, inviolable, and encourage clear unambiguous writing." There follow approximately 160 printed pages of simple, inviolable rules—which might lend credence to the view (albeit somewhat extreme) that house style is the accretion of the personal prejudices of generation upon generation of nit-picking

---

Does style matter?

- Style matters for its own sake; standards are important
- Style is necessary for the efficient dissemination of medical knowledge
- House style gives individual publications their identity
- Attention to style can count when it comes to having papers accepted

---

obsessionalists! Yet the *Economist* stylebook became a bestseller—so consistency, clarity, and accuracy (nit-picking?) must be widely recognised as desirable qualities in a piece of writing.

Style creates a favourable impression

These days, it seems, researchers are under great pressure to publish their work—careers and funding depend on publications as never before. Articles pour into journal offices. A few are of great scientific value, some are poor, and most are middling fair. Articles in the first two categories are generally easy to spot, but editors spend a great deal of time deciding which of the "middling" articles merit publication. Undoubtedly, good writing style and attention to detail can improve the chances of an "average" article being selected for publication.

Instructions to authors

Editors are human enough to be favourably impressed by a clear, easy to read paper whose authors have paid heed to the journal's instructions to contributors. Very few authors seem to read these. Journals do have different styles, which can be tedious for an author who has to rework an article each time it is submitted to a different journal. But it is sensible, and good manners, to set out a paper as requested and use the correct style for references and units (errors occur when results have to be converted and references changed from Harvard to Vancouver style or vice versa). All this effort also makes life less traumatic for authors, since even the most pedantic subeditor warms to the well presented paper and becomes more sparing in his or her use of the subeditorial pen.

Some elements of style

Good style, like good English, is not easy to define; and it is much easier to say what it *is not* than what it *is*. I will not discuss spelling, punctuation, or capitalisation here because these aspects of house style do not usually result in open warfare between the author and subeditor. More "creative" subediting may cause problems, however, so I have listed below some "do's" and "dont's" that should help reduce these.

103

Keep it short

- Editors are biased in favour of short articles (and short reference lists) as space is at a premium.
- If it is possible to cut out a word or sentence, always do so. "Now" is better than "at this moment in time," and "agreed" is better than "came to the identical conclusion."
- Sometimes whole paragraphs are redundant; the introduction often tells readers what they already know, and results should not be repeated in the discussion section.
- There is a law (somewhere) which states that the piece of prose of which you are most proud is probably the bit that should go first!

The longer the sentence the greater the likelihood of confusion

Long sentences can make laborious reading. "The relatively short duration of action on serum gastrin of SMS 201–995 when compared with omeprazole was also observed in our study since on the day after the five day treatment serum gastrin levels were increased due to the prolonged effects of omeprazole on gastrin release" is easier to follow if it is written as two sentences. "Our study also showed that the effect of SMS 201–995 on serum gastrin was not as long lasting as that of omeprazole. Serum gastrin concentrations were still high the day after a five day course of omeprazole treatment."

Syntax may go adrift in complicated sentences, tenses can become confused, and verbs and subjects may not agree when they have become lost or long separated in an overambitious construction.

Never use a long word when a short one will do

Writing scientific articles is not the same as writing "link lines" for Edwardian music hall. Long, complicated words will irritate rather than impress readers and do not make for easy reading.

Polysyllabic words do not have greater scientific credibility— "bifurcation" is not a more grown up word than "fork."

Avoid figures of speech and idiom

Scientific journals have an international readership. Write in a way that can be understood by someone whose first language is not English.

Passive constructions should be used sparingly

Use the active voice as it has greater impact and is more immediate. Remember, passive constructions can be very dull.

Avoid foreign, technical, or jargon words

If you can think of an ordinary English word use it. "The patient could walk" is better than "the patient was ambulatory"; "arms and legs" is preferable to "upper and lower extremities."

Words and phrases often used in medical conversation, such as "full work out" (investigation) and "blood sugar" (blood glucose concentration), are best avoided in writing.

Use abbreviations with care

● Abbreviations that are current in one country may not be recognised in another.

● Take a paper with lots of abbreviations, spell them all out in full, and some rather odd constructions may become evident.

● Well known abbreviations such as ECG, AIDS, and CT are permissible, but papers that are littered with unfamiliar, distracting abbreviations can be difficult to read.

● Always spell out an abbreviation the first time it is used.

Prepositions are better than strings of nouns

● Do not let a desire to cut words obscure the meaning of what you write.

● Lists of nouns (noun salads) as in the title "Doctor workload reduction programme" might cause difficulty to someone whose first language is not English; "Programme to reduce the workload of doctors" is longer but easier to understand.

Watch prefixes

The prefix "un" seems to be disappearing in favour of "non." Perhaps some people think that "non" has a more scientific air, but in many instances its use is incorrect. Thus we have "non-treated" patients, subjects given "non-necessary" drugs, and even "non-transplant immunological diseases."

Danglers

Make sure that modifying words and phrases refer clearly to the word modified. In the sentence, "Seven hundred and sixty patients were treated at St Mary's Hospital between 1964 and 1991 with azathioprine," poor old azathioprine is dangling around rather helplessly.

Participles do not provide a strong opening for sentences, and hanging participles, as the next sentence illustrates, lead to ambiguity: "Having a high temperature, one of us gave the patient a tepid bath" (the high temperature applies to "the patient" and not to "one of us").

Edit your own paper first

The job of the subeditor is to make the paper conform to the house style of the journal and to prepare the script for the printer. Contrary to the view of some authors, subeditors do not really like to rewrite, but sometimes this is necessary because of poor English or lack of clarity. Although it can be very annoying to have sections of a paper rewritten by a subeditor, especially if this seems to change the meaning, it is possible that the message was not absolutely clear in the first place.

Most of us have great difficulty in being objective about something we have written—because we know exactly what we mean, we imagine everyone else will. It may be worth trying to appraise an article from the viewpoint of a subeditor before it is submitted for publication.

● Distance yourself from your writing—do not look at it for a few days, then reconsider it stringently. Time can be a problem for those (most of us) who set deadlines then leave things until the last minute and do not have the few spare days required for this exercise.

● Record yourself reading the article aloud, then play back the recording. This should help to pinpoint any clumsy constructions.

● Ask a trusted friend or colleague to go through the paper querying points she or he does not fully understand; any ambiguity can then be rectified before the paper is subedited. (Let us hope the same can be said for the friendship.)

By this time you may be so bored by your article that you do not care what happens. Be resolute, be bold, post it . . . and remember Charles Lamb's words, "When my sonnet was rejected, I exclaimed, "Damn the age; I will write for Antiquity." That's style.

16 The future: electronic publishing

MAURICE LONG

It was commonly predicted in the early 1970s that by the end of the decade the traditional paper journal would have given way to the electronic journal. Looking back, those forecasts might seem ridiculous. Costs were prohibitive, computer and telecommunications technologies were in their infancy, and except for a small number of enthusiasts, few journal readers would have been prepared for the electronic journal. Even a decade later, in 1980, it seemed a long way off. What, then, has changed? Why are authors, librarians, and publishers now talking more earnestly than ever of "electronic publishing"?

The costs of computers and telecommunications have tumbled in the past 20 years; at the same time, the technology has advanced to a state where it is simple enough for all to use it—and an ever increasing number of people *want* to use it. It is the convergence of these developments that is rapidly altering the traditional model of disseminating scientific information.

Economics

Libraries have been suffering from a mixture of depressed acquisition funds and rising journal and book prices for some years. Librarians and publishers have different explanations for this state of affairs: one man's cause is another man's effect. Publishers believe declining library funds to be the real problem; funds for reading have not kept pace with funds for research. Librarians, on the other hand, are sure that the spiralling cost of journal subscriptions coupled with the exponential growth of new titles is the root cause of the problem.

This crisis in library acquisition funds has encouraged librarians to consider alternatives to the traditional paper journal. In particular, there is a trend to acquire journal articles when requested rather than "store" the journal issue: "just in time" as opposed to "just in case."

Technology

Acquiring journal articles as and when required rather than subscribing to rarely used journals is becoming easier because of the advances in information technology. The key developments have been in telecommunications and in laser and optical storage techniques. Throughout the 1970s and 1980s, libraries used computer databases to develop first local and then "networked" catalogues. Some of these cooperative catalogues have grown from academic library initiatives like OCLC in the United States, and others have been developed by national libraries such as the British Library, the National Library of Medicine, and INIST (France). Yet others have been built by the large learned societies, particularly in America.

National telecommunication networks such as the Internet in America and JANET in Britain have enabled librarians to quickly search references and order photocopies of required articles through the networks. In both North America and in continental Europe, telecommunication companies not known for their altruism are spending large sums of money on library research projects. Both library cooperatives and commercial document deliverers now have the ability to store images of journal articles and book chapters on optical disks, and these can be speedily delivered via the telecommunication network to the librarian or even the individual researcher. In general, publishers have been much slower to take advantage of these technology developments than their librarian customers. A few publishers, particularly in the United States, have instituted document delivery services. The only cooperative venture has been the ADONIS experiment; to date, this is showing only limited success. In using the new technologies, publishers may have been paying too much attention to the product, and not enough to the "market."

Culture

The market of the academic library and its users has gone through profound changes in the past five years.

108

The crisis in acquisition funding has led librarians to radically reconsider their role. In America, and increasingly in Europe, the old acquisition librarians are being rapidly replaced by the new breed of "collection development" librarians. Sophisticated computer software enables them to track very precisely the usage of individual journal titles. (Usage normally means requests for photocopies, rather than off the shelf browsing.) Since articles from rarely used, or even never used, journals can be obtained quickly through the network, the need to store the physical journal disappears. Describing themselves as information providers, rather than archivists, these librarians see the library providing a very different service than before. Some even talk about the emergence of the "virtual" library, where only essential journals and books are stored. Articles can be photocopied in a library perhaps thousands of miles away and delivered right to researchers' desktop fax machine or even, in full text ASCII format, to their PC's hard disk memory. Inside the library, the bibliophile is rapidly giving way to the information provider.

Perhaps even more significant is the emergence of a new type of library user—someone who has grown up with computer games and who is just as likely to search through teletext to determine television viewing than read a listings magazine will, if given the chance, "mouse" their way through a computer database to find the articles and references required in a particular research project. In undergraduate libraries awash with terminals, PCs, and compact disc readers, hard copy journal collections are going largely unused. The student is also more likely to generate written work on a word processor, with its vast memory and flexibility, than on a typewriter. If we can see the passing of the bibliophile librarian, it might be unrealistic to hope that the next generation of scientists will rescue the monograph or journal.

Economics, technology, and culture, all three; and the greatest of these is culture.

The new order

Publishers have been painfully aware of the difficult economic realities for some years, and they are beginning to realise that simply putting up journal subscription rates to counter falling subscriber numbers cannot be a long term solution. Some—a remarkably small number—have also been aware of some of the technology developments, although they have been applying this mainly to new print and production methods. They have not appreciated the effect those developments might already be having on their buyers (the librarians) and readers (students and researchers). Few science, technology, and medical (STM) publishers, however, have acknowledged the cultural sea changes taking place among those same audiences. For instance, most publishers would be reluctant to describe themselves as information brokers. Yet information rather than literature is largely what their readers are looking for. In many publishing houses there is an unconscious tension between the desire to produce a well turned out journal and the need to produce good "impact factor" ratings.

Perhaps it did not matter so much in the world of paper, but not recognising the importance and value of *information* might have disastrous results for traditional scientific publishers in the new world of *information technology*. The average high quality scientific journal might have ten key papers, each preceded by an abstract. It is estimated that no more than two articles in any issue will be of direct interest to even a committed journal reader or subscriber, although most of the abstracts will be "scanned" by the same reader. The researcher outside the discipline, who might refer to that journal once in a research project or perhaps only once in a lifetime of research, will have no commitment at all to the availability of the journal in paper format.

Library cooperative catalogues and network communication technologies make it easy for librarians to access and acquire the article or abstract that a student or researcher needs. The only questions that remain are who should provide the information delivery service and how to put a monetary value on such purchases. The answer to the first question will probably be provided by market conditions and technology developments. The harder question is: what is the financial value of these "bits" of information?

Who pays?

This leads directly to the discussion of the nature of publishing itself. This is not a new discussion. The nailing of a thesis to a church or university door and passing it around a group of scholars has its present day analogue in the "grey literature" and, more recently, in the academic electronic bulletin boards. Is this publishing? In replying "not really," the traditional STM publisher would argue that the modern scientific journal has the added value of rigorous peer review.

Few would dispute that the peer review process adds a special value to the published research. In paper format, this extra value can be directly related to the subscription cost for the journal. Its value is what the publisher says it is, and in the main, the publisher has been helped by copyright laws, at least in developed countries. Previously produced and distributed only in print format, the journal can *now* be stored and replicated electronically by others, and distributed to customers who may or may not want to pay the primary publisher. In the United States, the National Library of Medicine delivers an estimated 186 000 documents each year, free of any royalty to the primary publisher. The number of image documents supplied in the United States was believed to be in excess of 6·9 million in the academic year 1989–1990.[1] In only a fraction of cases were royalties paid either directly to the publisher or through the Copyright Clearance Center.

There seems little doubt that the decline of journal subscription numbers and eventually the fall in the number of new paper journals will be balanced by the growth of alternative information delivery methods. Nobody is forecasting a decline in the output of scientific research. But it is clear that much work will need to be done to establish new payment models, and a number of interesting experiments are appearing, especially in North Amercia.

It is quite likely that primary publishers will use the computer and telecommunication developments to stimulate demand for scientific papers in advance of publication, developing their own current awareness services among groups of interested scientists. Early notice might be given by posting the titles of accepted papers to the networks; the "market" could be further stimulated by electronically distributing the abstract to perhaps a smaller group of potential readers. Finally, either the image of the article or its ASCII text could be made available at the same time as the paper journal issue appears. The printed version could itself be formatted on the screen and printer in the library or at the researcher's desk to look like a traditional printed page. It seems inevitable that there will be closer cooperation between the primary publishers and the library networking systems in delivering scientific information.

Indeed, many of these systems are already in place; working out pricing models might take a little while. It is quite likely, however, that in future we will see a considerable increase in the price of buying a single abstract or article, matched, perhaps, by a compensating decline in the cost of the paper "archival" journal issue. For paper journals will undoubtedly survive, though perhaps in fewer numbers. Probably, the more general a journal is in its field, the more it will be valued as a wide information source by its readers.

Whatever happens, STM publishers, both commercial houses and learned societies, who wish to survive will need to adapt quickly to the new order.

The author

We have looked in some depth at the effects the economic, technological, and cultural changes are having on libraries and publishers. How will they affect the author?

In preparing his or her paper, most scientific authors are already using the technology for research, and usually that research is written up on word processors. Chemists, physicists, and mathematicians already use special word processing software that can handle numbers, formulas, and symbols. For the rest, standard packages are more than adequate. Increasingly, publishers are asking authors to send in the disk together with the revised manuscript.

But the new technologies also allow the author the kind of direct access to readers and colleagues which was impossible just a few years ago. Authors can communicate via electronic mail and bulletin boards with colleagues and have their research published after peer review in non-paper electronic journals for small interest groups. For a wider audience, papers published in traditional paper journals can be simultaneously distributed around the networks and accessed easily and specifically by those for whom it is relevant. Is this not the primary purpose of publishing the results of scientific research?

---

[1] Kutz M. Estimate of the size of the document delivery market in the United States. Paper presented to the Associaton of American Publishers. February, 1992.

Index